Cambridge Elements ☰

Elements in the Philosophy of Biology
edited by
Grant Ramsey
KU Leuven

HUMAN COGNITIVE DIVERSITY

Ingo Brigandt
University of Alberta

CAMBRIDGE
UNIVERSITY PRESS

Shaftesbury Road, Cambridge CB2 8EA, United Kingdom

One Liberty Plaza, 20th Floor, New York, NY 10006, USA

477 Williamstown Road, Port Melbourne, VIC 3207, Australia

314–321, 3rd Floor, Plot 3, Splendor Forum, Jasola District Centre,
New Delhi – 110025, India

103 Penang Road, #05–06/07, Visioncrest Commercial, Singapore 238467

Cambridge University Press is part of Cambridge University Press & Assessment,
a department of the University of Cambridge.

We share the University's mission to contribute to society through the pursuit of
education, learning and research at the highest international levels of excellence.

www.cambridge.org
Information on this title: www.cambridge.org/9781009496414

DOI: 10.1017/9781009496407

First published 2025

A catalogue record for this publication is available from the British Library

ISBN 978-1-009-49641-4 Hardback
ISBN 978-1-009-49636-0 Paperback
ISSN 2515-1126 (online)
ISSN 2515-1118 (print)

Human Cognitive Diversity

Elements in the Philosophy of Biology

DOI: 10.1017/9781009496407
First published online: August 2025

Ingo Brigandt
University of Alberta

Author for correspondence: Ingo Brigandt, brigandt@ualberta.ca

Abstract: We humans are diverse. But how to understand human diversity in the case of cognitive diversity? This Element discusses how to properly investigate human behavioural and cognitive diversity, how to scientifically represent, and how to explain cognitive diversity. Since there are various methodological approaches and explanatory agendas across the cognitive and behavioural sciences, which can be more or less useful for understanding human diversity, a critical analysis is needed. And as the controversial study of sex and gender differences in cognition illustrates, the scientific representations and explanations put forward matter to society and impact public policy, including policies on mental health. But how to square the vision of human cognitive diversity with the assumption that we all share one human nature? Is cognitive diversity something to be positively valued? The author engages with these questions in connection with the issues of neurodiversity, cognitive disability, and essentialist construals of human nature.

Keywords: human cognitive diversity, neurodiversity, gender differences in cognition, science, values, and society, methods and research agendas in cognitive science

ISBNs: 9781009496414 (HB), 9781009496360 (PB), 9781009496407 (OC)
ISSNs: 2515-1126 (online), 2515-1118 (print)

Contents

1 Introduction

Life on our planet is diverse. Not only is there diversity between species, but there is phenotypic diversity within any species. We, humans, are a particularly diverse species, especially regarding our behaviour, language, and cognition. Having generated our distinctive ecological niches through cultural evolution and social, institutional, and technological innovations, we have created diverse ways of experiencing and interacting with each other, and continually transform the behaviour and cognition exhibited across individuals. But how to understand such between-person cognitive diversity? How can and should we scientifically investigate and explain human cognitive variation? And is cognitive diversity something to be appreciated and valued? After all, the roots of human behaviour and the idea of cognitive differences between groups of people have been subject to thorny nature-nurture disputes. So what are the societal stakes for the scientific study of human cognitive variation? And how to square the reality and significance of human cognitive diversity with the common idea that we all share one nature, including a shared cognitive architecture?

In my longstanding work in the philosophy of biology, I have engaged with the evolution and development of the various phenotypes and life-forms seen across the animal kingdom. With this Cambridge Element, my focus turns from life to mind. The basic question to be pursued is how to investigate, scientifically represent, explain, and appreciate human cognitive and behavioural diversity. Beyond the scientific study of human cognition in the cognitive and behavioural sciences, my discussion will engage with the societal implications of such scientific research and how we ought to think about cognitive diversity across persons. Unlike the more neutral term 'cognitive variation,' I employ the notion of cognitive diversity in line with my position that cognitive variation is something to be positively valued.

Sections 2 and 3 of this Cambridge Element focus on the scientific study of human cognition, the former section discussing how to *scientifically represent* cognitive diversity and the latter turning to the question of how to *explain* cognitive diversity. There already are various approaches and methodological perspectives used within the cognitive and behavioural sciences, which I will critically discuss with an eye on which are more conducive to capturing the full range and nature of human cognitive diversity. In a nutshell, I contrast approaches that are primarily investigating cognitive *difference* between groups of people with research that has the potential to capture cognitive *diversity*. Although research on cognitive differences between races is not scientifically reputable any longer, research on sex and gender differences in cognition is quite active, and hence will be one focus of my critical scrutiny. (My methodological criticism still carries over to other categories than gender, including race.) Comparing this with other approaches in cognitive science, Section 2 also addresses how the investigative methodologies, the analytical categories, and the representational frameworks used by cognitive science researchers matter to society, for example, by avoiding scientific representations and communications that reinforce harmful stereotypes about groups of persons. Then Section 3 turns to various methodological approaches for explaining cognitive diversity. While research on sex differences in the brain focuses on the biological basis of cognitive differences, there are various approaches in the cognitive and behavioural sciences that also capture the impact of social-environmental factors on cognition. Explanatory frameworks that capture the mutual interaction of neurocognitive and social-environmental processes better convey to the public that the present shape of human cognitive diversity is contingent and in flux. And for such social-political purposes as improving mental health – while also reducing social inequities in mental health – scientific explanations that include the role of socio-environmental factors are better positioned to suggest social policy options.

The question of how to properly appreciate human cognitive diversity, including the very ideas of *neurodiversity* and *human nature*, is the topic of Section 4. Beyond my earlier critical scrutiny of scientific approaches, now I will examine the natural goodness account in neo-Aristotelian ethics (as a contemporary tradition beyond the philosophy of science). I reject this account due to its inherent ableism (including about cognitive disabilities) and its endorsement of a species-universal standard for bodily and cognitive functioning that is at odds with human diversity. In contrast, my emphasis on the diversity of cognitive functioning is more in line with the neurodiversity paradigm, which views various non-neurotypical conditions (e.g., ADHD and autism) as part of normal human cognitive diversity. Given that the notion of human nature often suggests one biological nature shared by all humans (e.g., evolutionary psychology postulating a universal cognitive architecture), this raises the question of whether we should employ the concept of human nature at all. I conclude by arguing that if one is to endorse the idea of human nature, it needs to be an account of human nature that sufficiently captures human cognitive diversity and that does not dehumanize some of us by adopting a normative construal of human nature that would proclaim certain traits as normal or essential for having a fully human nature.

2 Representing Human Cognitive Diversity

The topic of this section is how to properly investigate and represent the presence of human cognitive variation. My strategy is to critically contrast research approaches that are primarily after cognitive *difference* (i.e., differences between groups of persons) with approaches that are better poised to capture the full range and *diversity* of human cognition. Laying out the inadequacies of the former approaches juxtaposed with the benefits of the latter serves as a useful pointer to proper methodologies to represent cognitive variation. To be sure, this contrast is too schematic to do justice to the full shape of existing research approaches. But my discussion will also make clear that within sex-difference research there are several perspectives; and when covering various approaches that tend to be conducive to investigating cognitive diversity, I also point to their limitations.

The study of cognitive differences between races has become scientifically disreputable and has been abandoned by mainstream cognitive and behavioural science. In contrast, research on cognitive differences between women and men is a comparatively active area (Halpern 2012; Hamilton 2008; Hines 2004; Ruigrok et al. 2014). Some researchers even talk about 'the female brain' as opposed to 'the male brain' (Baron-Cohen 2003). While in the case of race, it has been recognized that there are no genetic boundaries setting races apart that could account for clear cognitive differences (Gannett 2004; Kaplan and Winther 2013), one motivation for still pursuing cognitive science on sex differences appears to be that many such researchers feel that there are real, biological differences between women and men, for example, in terms of different sex chromosomes and sex hormone levels (as Section 3 will critically engage with). Because of its relative prominence, my presentation of approaches interested in revealing cognitive difference focuses on research on sex and gender differences. Just like in the outdated case of race, we will see that such research has not only empirical and methodological flaws, but can also have problematic social effects, so from the social-political value of equity, research that captures cognitive diversity is preferable.

2.1 Research on Sex Differences in the Brain

Many neuroscientists and cognitive scientists investigating the role of biological sex often call their field 'the study of sex differences in the brain' (Becker et al. 2007; McCarthy et al. 2012). This designation indicates that a central *aim* of such research is to reveal cognitive difference. (We will later see how this differs from aiming at an understanding of cognitive diversity.) The main theoretical framework in this domain is the *organizational-activational hypothesis*, which asserts that differential exposure to steroid hormones – often referred to as sex hormones – influences brain development in a dimorphic fashion (Arnold 2009). First, during in-utero development, prenatal levels of sex hormones are said to 'organize' the brains of male and female mammals in a different fashion, and later, for example, during puberty or adulthood, released sex hormones 'activate' these brain regions, resulting in different behaviour in males and females. Testosterone is the hormone deemed to drive male brain differentiation, whereas estrogen is the hormone underlying female brain development.

A substantial amount of research on sex differences in the brain focuses on non-human mammals, with rodents used as a model permitting experimental investigation. In this context, claims about sex-specific neurophysiology can be limited to reproductive behaviour (and the underlying brain regions). In contrast, the most controversial scientific accounts claim various cognitive capacities and gender-stereotypical behaviours to occur in a sex-dimorphic fashion, including verbal abilities, spatial reasoning, mathematical abilities, nurturing behaviours, and sexual orientation. (Although the latter is claimed to be a heterosexual orientation for either sex, this counts as dimorphic as women are seen as being neurophysiologically disposed to be attracted *to men*, whereas men are attracted *to women*.) Such an account is also called *brain organization theory* (Jordan-Young 2010). Psychologist Simon Baron-Cohen (2003), neuropsychiatrist Louann Brizendine (2006, 2010), and psychologist Susan Pinker (2008) even talk about this alleged dimorphism in terms of 'the male brain' as opposed to 'the female brain.'

These researchers want a label like 'male brain' to be understood as more than a classificatory concept that describes a correlation of neurophysiological or cognitive traits present in men. For it is taken to be an explanatory theory, which posits that this correlation is explained by the previous presence of high levels of testosterone. But note that then one has to provide evidence for this explanatory cause over and above the phenomenon to be explained. This makes it much more demanding to support the theory of the male brain than merely documenting some correlation of cognitive traits and calling this 'the male brain' – as it also happens.[1] I'll get in a second to whether the very correlation of cognitive traits deemed characteristic of men and a different trait-correlation characteristic of women exists. But Baron-Cohen (2003) also uses purely speculative evolutionary psychology considerations to argumentatively bolster his dimorphic vision that the male brain is about *systemizing*, whereas the female

---

[1] Ridley (2019) makes a similar critical point about Baron-Cohen's (2002) 'extreme male brain' theory of autism. Pondering whether 'extreme male brain' is a descriptor or an explanation, Ridley makes plain that Baron-Cohen cannot point to the mere presence of certain behavioural traits (more pronouncedly present in autistic men than in neurotypical men) as establishing the notion of an extreme male brain, when the latter is also taken as an explanatory theory of these behavioural traits in terms of underlying neurophysiological properties.

brain is for *emphasizing*. Evolutionary psychologists tend to adopt the vision of a 'monomorphic mind,' that is, a universally shared cognitive architecture among humans, which evolved as the best adaptation to our Pleistocene social environment (Buller 2005, 2006) – Section 3.2 will explain how this is at odds with the genetic and phenotypic variation known from evolutionary biology. The one exception within this monomorphism approach is a dimorphism between the sexes. Baron-Cohen (2003, 117) proclaims that the male brain and the female brain are adaptations to two different ecological niches ("our male and female ancestors occupied quite different niches"). However, there could have been two *separate* ecological niches only if being able to *both* systemize and emphasize well had yielded in past social environments a lower biological fitness than the fitness of someone who could only systemize as well as the fitness of someone who could only emphasize. But this is contradicted by Baron-Cohen acknowledging that some persons indeed have a balanced brain (brain-type B), that is, being good at systematizing as well as empathizing. Baron-Cohen's evolutionary psychology claim is yet again an explanatory model (explaining alleged cognitive patterns in extant humans) for which one would have to provide evidence, in this case, evidence pertaining to the evolutionary past – over and above evidence for the pattern to be explained. My impression is that this is one of many instances where an evolutionary psychology story (actually devoid of historical support) is not so much put forward as a historical account, but rhetorically deployed in an attempt to fill evidential gaps about a claimed *current* cognitive situation (e.g., a sex-specific correlation of cognitive capacities) or about its claimed underlying mechanistic basis (e.g., a sex hormone generating this correlation; Brigandt 2024b).

Despite the presence of researchers in some parts of behavioural science who endorse brain organization theory in the case of humans and actively investigate sex differences in the brain, there have been substantial criticisms about the evidential support of brain organization theory (Fine 2010, 2017; Joel and Vikhanski 2019; Jordan-Young and Rumiati 2012; Rippon 2019). Many critiques target the alleged evidence for sex hormones being the main driver of the formation of either a female brain or a male brain, but some engage with the empirical support for the very presence of the package of cognitive traits deemed to characterize either brain type. A landmark in this respect is the book-length treatment by Rebecca Jordan-Young (2010), surveying the scientific literature available at the time. Brain organization theory posits a correlation between features of cognition (e.g., language lateralization, verbal abilities, and visuo-spatial abilities), personality and interests, sexual orientation, as well as handedness across women – and another correlation pattern for men. (Handedness is part of the theoretical prediction since left-handedness is associated with unusual hormone exposures.) Among other things, Jordan-Young argues that when incorporating the various studies available in the analysis (as opposed to cherry-picking those that support brain organization theory), most of the posited correlations do not exist. Based on a meta-analysis, psychologist Janet Hyde (2005) likewise challenges the idea of substantial gender differences in cognition and instead proposes her gender similarities hypothesis.

These are important *empirical* critiques, but the topic of my discussion is not theories (and their truth or falsity) but *methodologies* that guide investigation and the formation of scientific representations – and how adequate such methodologies are and whether there are better ones. In the present case, we are focusing on scientific approaches whose central *agenda or aim* is to reveal sex differences in cognition. One implication of using such a methodological orientation is a publication bias. If a study finds some of the sought-after differences between women and men (in a statistically significant fashion), this is widely reported. But if some research yields data that fails to document such differences (and thus suggests that there are not any systematic differences between women and men), this is often not deemed worthy of publication in a scientific journal, generating a bias toward the reporting of positive findings at the expense of negative findings. Yet my discussion centres on the methodological characteristic stemming from aiming at cognitive differences that I call adopting a *typological approach*, by seeking to uncover a female condition and a male condition (each consisting of a package of neurocognitive traits) and representing findings in these terms. This is an impoverished investigative and analytical framework, as variation with an analytical category such as sex or gender (i.e., cognitive variation among women) is not of genuine interest, forming a methodological approach producing a *representational inadequacy*.

I take over the label 'typological' approach from scientific criticisms of typological thinking about biological species (Brigandt 2024a). Typological thinking postulates a species type while ignoring the importance of variation between individuals within a species. In contrast, modern evolutionary biology favours population thinking, according to which the traits of individuals are primary, and trait mean values are merely a statistical derivation from the features of individuals – where the trait mean is also subject to evolutionary change (Mayr 1959). Within-population variation is important to evolutionary theory because natural selection can only act on phenotypic variation and because genetic variation makes gradual evolutionary change possible. Sober (1980) diagnoses the contrary typological thinking – which is also called essentialism about species – as the adoption of a natural state model, analogous to how Aristotelian physics assumed that objects on the Earth (in the sublunary sphere) have a natural state to which they tend to move (as an instance of natural motion), unless they are subjected to intervening forces. This analysis makes it plain that when engaging in typological thinking about species, one can *acknowledge* the presence of variation between individuals – which is readily observable – while not deeming this variation of any importance. Such research is about finding a species' type, whereas variation is seen to merely consist in deviations from this type, due to interfering forces (e.g., environmental fluctuations) that are of scant scientific interest.

A typological approach – regarding gender or sex differences – is clearly adopted by those accounts that talk about the female brain and the male brain. This methodological and analytical orientation persists even when it is acknowledged that not every woman has a female brain. For instance, the prominent researcher Simon Baron-Cohen (2003, 2) attempts to absolve himself by mentioning that he is "not talking about all females: just about the average female, compared to the average male. Empathy is a skill (or a set of skills). As with any other skill … we all vary in it."[2] But he goes on to constantly present (alleged) findings in terms of the male brain and the female brain, also talking about "the brain *type E* (for empathizing)" and "the male brain *type S* (for systemizing)" (2003, 3 & 4) – as if such a reified female brain type was more real or important than a woman's actual cognitive properties (that hardly ever matches the average). Just like in the case of typological thinking about biological species, when setting out to find what the two brain types are, a typological approach to genders or sexes also permits one to acknowledge within-group variation, while not deeming it of genuine scientific importance. This typological vision is spread further by Baron-Cohen talking on several occasions about the 'essential' differences between the female and the male brain, and by him declaring the female brain type and the male brain type to be adaptations to two distinct niches. This promotes the interpretation that when a woman does not accord with the female brain type (or average), she should be seen as performing above (or below) her brain type – as if conforming to the type was a legitimate expectation.

Even when staying clear of talking about the 'essential difference' in the minds of women and men, a good deal of research focused on cognitive differences is not aimed at investigating within-gender cognitive variation (and explaining this variation), but is primarily interested in representing findings in terms of a female condition and a male condition. Such a typological approach is often indicated by talk in terms of 'sex-specific' neurocognitive properties. One instructive case in

---

[2] Likewise, Pinker (2008, 95) states that "women, on average, have a small but distinct empathy advantage" and Brizendine (2006) talks about women, on average, differing from men. However, they also juxtapose this with a presentation in terms of the female brain and the male brain, which dominates their discussions.

point is McCarthy et al. (2017), a review article on the role of neuroepigenetics and neuroimmunology in the establishment of sex differences in the brain. While also using experimental findings from rodent models, these researchers argue for the importance of investigating sex differences in human neuropsychiatry, motivated by an overview of nearly two dozen neuropsychiatric, neurological, and neurodegenerative conditions, showing in each case sex differences in prevalence, onset, and phenotype between women and men. In line with a typological approach, their figure 3 on inflammatory responses and synaptic patterning depicts nothing but one male condition and one female condition for causal pathways, contributing to "Sex-specific adult behaviours" in rodents (McCarthy et al. 2017, 477). Beyond the genetically standardized lab animals kept in a controlled environment, this account glosses over the neurophysiological variation present in rodents from natural populations; and the use of typological representational framework is certainly problematic for the ultimate research target of *human* neuropsychiatry. Although this is simply a schematic image in a review article, a good deal of research on sex differences in human neurocognition is after such findings that are analyzed and represented in this typological fashion.

The reason why I single out McCarthy et al. (2017) as noteworthy is that this research is about the role of *epigenetics*. Epigenetic modifications, such as DNA methylations and histone modifications, do not alter the nucleotide sequence of DNA and thus do not impact the protein produced by a gene. But epigenetic modifications have an important biological role as they can upregulate or downregulate the transcription of a gene and thereby impact a particular gene's activity in certain tissues, including neurons in the brain. Since epigenetic modifications result from signals in a cell's or organism's environment, epigenetics has often been hailed as offering a mechanistic link between environmental and neurophysiological features, capturing the role of the human social environment including a person's experiences and past behaviour (Powledge 2011; Read et al. 2009; Toyokawa et al. 2012). Consequently, as Sarah Richardson (2017) has argued, epigenetics research could investigate how environmental conditions create *variation* in some sex-stereotyped behaviour across females and across males – which from my perspective would mean eschewing a typological approach. However, Richardson discusses several cases where some researchers instead view epigenetic plasticity as sexually dimorphic and focus on finding and representing *sex-specific* responses to the environment (deemed to stem from male- and female-specific epigenetic profiles). I point to McCarthy et al. (2017) as another example where epigenetics is not used to investigate and represent variation, but juxtaposed with (and possibly distorted by) a typological approach – and there are other such examples driven by the aim of studying sex differences (e.g., Chung and Auger 2013; McCarthy et al. 2009; Qureshi and Mehler 2010).

Not all of the researchers investigating sex or gender differences in cognition explicitly adopt or tacitly operate with a typological approach. But deploying a typological approach is an inadequate methodology regarding *investigation as well as data analysis and representation*. If a study's exclusive aim is to uncover sex or gender differences, then the full range and distribution of cognitive variation that is actually present within any sex or within any gender is not being investigated (Section 2.2 will momentarily point to some other approaches that fare better in studying variation.) And to the extent to which significant data on neurocognitive traits across individuals is present, accounts operating with a typological approach will primarily conduct kinds of data analysis that capture cognitive differences between women and men, for example, tracking down those neurocognitive traits that show a statistically significant difference. Likewise, scientific representations developed or disseminated will convey the female and the male average, often without indicating the extent and nature of variation across any average. Moreover, in the case of research that is primarily after sex or gender differences, only one primary analytical category (be it sex or gender) is being used. This is methodologically inadequate as data is not being gathered or analyzed concerning other possible analytical categories and, more problematically, the use of one category erroneously suggests that this one category is somehow scientifically privileged or more real than variation concerning any other analytical dimension. We have also seen that talking in terms of a female brain type as opposed to a male brain type (or a female brain and a male brain) tends to promote the (mis)interpretation that cognitive trait averages – reified as types – are more representative than the actual traits of individuals. In Section 2.3, I will address that, beyond scientific research, a typological methodology also has problematic societal impacts. But first I point to alternative methodological approaches that are more conducive to capturing diversity.

2.2 How to Properly Investigate and Represent Cognitive Diversity

As previously documented, the psychologist Baron-Cohen (2003) adopts a typological approach by focusing on the notion of a female brain type as opposed to a male brain type. He occasionally hints at the presence of variation, by acknowledging that he is more precisely referring to an average across women and an average across men. But even consistently talking in terms of averages is methodologically insufficient. For one thing, one also would have to detail the particular range and shape of variation. More importantly, an average pertains to a *single* cognitive ability (or a single neurophysiological trait). This raises the question of how to investigate various neurocognitive traits and their relations. Brain organization theory posits a clear correlation among several cognitive capacities and tendencies for women (including high verbal fluency, high nurturing tendency, low spatial reasoning, and low mathematical ability) and a correlation among different traits for men. Indeed, the notion of a female brain and a male brain implies the presence of a package of traits characteristic of women and another trait package for men. An alternative and very different vision is the *mosaic brain hypothesis* proposed by the neuroscientist Daphna Joel. While she originally introduced the mosaic brain under the label of 'intersex brain' (Joel 2011), from the outset she has made clear that we cannot even view human neurocognition as consisting of a linear continuum with the female brain and the male brain located toward the outer ends. Framing their approach as an alternative to a sex-difference approach, Joel and Fausto-Sterling (2016) point out that documenting more and more neurocognitive traits that are either more common in women (and in this sense more typical of women) or more typical of men does not lend increasing empirical support for the existence of the female and the male brain. For it is still possible that most women are a mosaic of some traits that are more common among women combined with some other traits that are more typical of men, with most men likewise being a mosaic of female-typical and male-typical traits. The set of traits found together in a particular person may well differ from person to person, so that there are no simple package deals of different traits that are typically correlated.

Joel and her collaborators have adduced evidence in support of the mosaic brain hypothesis (Joel 2021; Joel et al. 2015, 2018; Joel and Vikhanski 2019). The hypothesis has also been criticized, primarily based on the argument that upon analyzing several cognitive traits of a person one can still fairly reliably infer whether this is from a woman or a man (Chekroud et al. 2016). As I have said before, my primary focus is not on empirical matters such as the truth of the mosaic brain hypothesis. Instead, I point to it as suggesting a *methodological* approach to investigating, analyzing, and representing human cognition. The methodological guideline is to investigate a large number of neurophysiological and cognitive variables, uncovering for each of them specific values across various persons. An analysis and scientific representation of such data would chart joint probability distributions across such neurocognitive variables, such as mapping out that when having some specific neurocognitive properties, there is a particular probability of having some set of other neurocognitive traits, while other sets of traits are also possible, each with a certain frequency. Finding out about such complex distributions of various properties is scientifically very demanding. But at minimum, a methodological approach that aims at investigating and representing human cognitive diversity – rather than merely finding a cognitive difference between two groups of persons – will analyze data not only in terms of a single analytical category (such as sex or gender), but with respect to several analytical categories and thus along *several* dimensions of cognitive variation.

One important dimension of cognitive variation is culture. This is the province of the field of *cultural psychology* (Cohen and Kitayama 2019; Fernández and Evans 2022; Gelfand et al. 2013). Although this field has its roots in some twentieth-century psychology, influential for the formation of contemporary cultural psychology has been the work by Richard Nisbett (2005), focusing on the ways in which Asians and Westerners differ in their modes of thought. For instance, East Asians tend to use a more holistic style of thinking, compared to the analytical style of Westerners. The former style pays attention to an entire field and assigns causality to it (also tending to favour a dialectical mode of reasoning), while the latter focuses on objects and assigns dispositions to them, when also reasoning in terms of logical rules (Nisbett et al. 2001). This is hypothesized to stem from longstanding differences in social organizations across such cultures. It has also been argued that the way that artistic styles differ, for example, as reflected in images created, results from culturally modulated variation in attention (as measured by eye-tracking), among other psychological factors (Masuda et al. 2008).

An important agenda has been set out and pursued by anthropologist, psychologist, and human evolutionary biologist Joseph Henrich. Henrich's starting point is psychology's traditional experimental focus on WEIRD people – which is his acronym for people from Western, educated, industrialized, rich, and democratic countries, while also flagging that this type of cognition is an outlier. Not only has most psychological research been conducted in Western countries, but the research participants providing data are typically college undergraduates, often psychology majors. (Henrich et al. 2010 estimate that 96 percent of study samples come from countries that taken together have only 12 percent of the global population.) Given the received assumption that a good deal of human cognition – at least basic cognitive architecture – is universal, such a sample bias may not seem problematic at all. And even when not making bold claims about universality, psychologists often assume that the results of their cognitive studies generalize well past their research participants.

Henrich et al. (2010) challenge this universality assumption by documenting significant differences in cognition and reasoning between industrialized and non-industrialized societies, between Western and non-Western societies, and between US Americans and the rest of the West. Among other aspects of cognition, these divergences include decision-making about cooperation and punishment, motivations to conform, folkbiological reasoning, self-views and the use of self-concepts (independent or interdependent), as well as spatial cognition, for example, using an egocentric spatial system. Particularly striking is that cross-cultural comparison shows that there is variation in being subject to the Müller-Lyer optical illusion, with some people from some non-Western cultures not being prone to the illusion and instead perceiving the two arrows as of identical length. Fodor (1983) prominently argued that visual systems are informationally encapsulated (i.e., cognitively impenetrable) – in which case there could not be any culturally modulated cognitive influence on optical illusions. But it turns out that even such seemingly basic cognitive processes as vision vary across persons from different cultures (McCauley and Henrich 2006). Henrich et al. (2010) also document that the WEIRD psychology found in college undergraduates is not as common in less-educated US Americans and that such cognitive variations aligning with socio-economic status (SES) are even found in children. This shows that there is cognitive variation even within one culture; and contemporary Americans are psychologically WEIRDer than their forebears from a century ago, indicating a cultural change in cognition across history. Beyond using such already documented differences to make the point that WEIRD people are actually a cognitive minority globally, Henrich et al.'s perspective calls for additional, detailed cultural psychology investigations as to how various aspects of cognition and emotion vary within and across cultures.[3]

Although slightly younger than cultural psychology, alongside is the field of cultural neuroscience. In addition to studying cognition and emotion, cultural neuroscience investigates the underlying neuroanatomy and neurophysiology – especially how these features vary across cultures (Chiao 2009; Chiao et al. 2013; Choudhury and Slaby 2012; Kim and Sasaki 2014; Losin et al. 2010). There are cases where for the same psychological task, people from different cultures still use different neurophysiological processes and even different brain regions. For instance, native Chinese and English speakers engage different neural regions when performing an identical arithmetical task (Tang et al. 2006). And when empathizing with familiar persons who make angry facial expressions, Chinese and German study participants tend to deploy different brain regions (de Greck et al. 2012). Although recruiting the same brain region, when observing the emotional pain of in-group as opposed to out-group

---

[3] Section 3.2 will lay out how Henrich (2020) intends to explain the historical change in cognition and the very advent of the WEIRD psychology.

members, there is still a different level of neuronal activation in Koreans as compared to European Americans (Cheon et al. 2011).

An example of cultural neuroscience that correlates cultural variation in psychology with variation in underlying brain processes deals with the role of oxytocin, which is produced in the hypothalamus. Functioning as a neuro-transmitter as well as a hormone, oxytocin is deemed to promote prosocial attitudes and behaviours, maybe by increasing an individual's sensitivity to salient social cues (Kim and Sasaki 2014). Since it is known that human populations living in regions with higher pathogen exposure develop more collectivistic (or even tribalistic) cultures with stronger in-group biases and more intolerant attitudes to out-group members (Fincher et al. 2008), oxytocin is likely involved in neurophysiological processes that vary across cultures. Biological traits that are not present within the brain can also inform cultural neuroscience research. A case in point is proinflammatory cytokines, whose deployment as part of a person's immune response can have beneficial results in the short term, but in the long term can lead to chronic inflammation. It is well-known that people from some cultures are less likely to solicit explicit social support, as they are concerned about perturbing their social network. Comparing Asian and European Americans, Chiang et al. (2012) have investigated cultural variation in the connection between a person's perception of the availability of supportive relationships and their levels of the proinflammatory cytokine interleukin-6.

Chiang et al.'s (2012) comparison of Asian Americans and European Americans also illustrates the existence of research on variation within one country, so as to go beyond contrasting geographically distant cultures. Another example is Cohen et al. (1996), who have studied regional differences within the US by comparing southern and northern men regarding how they respond to insults, in this case tracking variation in the hormones cortisol and testosterone associated with aggression. Cognitive variation within other cultures or regions such as Japan or Turkey's Black Sea region has likewise been investigated (Kitayama et al. 2006; Uskul et al. 2008). One way to neurocognitively investigate variation within a country is in terms of social class, for example, by comparing educated with less-educated persons or middle-class with working-class persons (Snibbe and Markus 2005; Stephens et al. 2007). Also investigating the role of the hormone cortisol, Stephens et al. (2012) have compared first-generation college students, who face more psychological challenges adjusting to school life, with continuing-generation students. In addition to traditional explanations of this heightened challenge such as limited finances and academic preparation, they argue that a psychological aspect of the explanation is a cultural mismatch, where first-generation college students socialized by interdependent norms face the independent middle-class norms that dominate college life. Religion is another category that permits the investigation of culturally related cognitive variation within a country alone (Cohen and Hill 2007).[4]

At the same time, there are limitations and pitfalls for any approach attempting to study neurocognitive diversity, including in the larger domains of cultural psychology and cultural neuroscience (Bao and Pöppel 2012; Martínez Mateo et al. 2012; see also Packer and Cole 2023). Above all, merely contrasting Westerners and East Asians is conceptually too schematic and can prompt a typological interpretation that – analogous to the typological approach to gender and cognition criticized in the previous subsection – misconstrues each cultural group as being cognitively homogenous (each having one 'typical' style of reasoning). For example, as Martínez Mateo et al. (2013) point out, in a cultural neuroscience study focusing on Chinese study participants, Zhang et al. (2006) talk about "the Chinese self" uncovered by fMRI brain imaging. Wang et al. (2012) similarly refer to their Chinese participants as having "collectivistic brains." Although by now various individual studies have accumulated that, taken together, study many different cultures and other groups (and also document some variation within cultures), we still have to go beyond the impression created by the traditional focus on comparing Westerners and Asians (Masuda et al. 2020). Apart from potentially obscuring variation within a culture, a contrastive comparison of two cultures or geographic regions can also promote a binary interpretation of possible modes of cognition (Martínez Mateo et al. 2013). Contrasting a collectivistic psychology with an individualistic psychology or contrasting a holistic style of reasoning with an analytic style fails to make explicit that each psychological 'style' consists of several distinct cognitive and behavioural traits, which differ between persons to create various intermediate and alternative individual psychologies not confirming to a binary.

Another challenge is to standardize the various analytical categories that are being used by studies around the globe, such as culture, gender, race, ethnicity, SES, and education. (Gatzke-Kopp 2016 points out that many studies do not report the race or SES of their participants at all.) Vogeley and Roepstorff (2009) also argue that culture is a dynamic entity subject to looping effects (see Hacking 1999), so that 'culture' cannot be construed as a simple

---

[4] Apart from mapping out cognitive variation along culture and the like, cognitive differences across individuals matter for psychology in other ways (Seghier and Price 2018; Ward 2022). There are also interesting questions about whether cognitive differences are quantitative or qualitative in character, or whether behavioural differences are merely prompted by different social environments acting on largely identical psychologies or due to deeper differences between psychologies (Rouder and Haaf 2021; Schulz 2023).

analytical category or external variable that can be measured and then taken to be fixed. Regarding practical (rather than conceptual) challenges, an obvious hurdle for cross-cultural research is to obtain a sufficient number and spread of samples to arrive at study participants that are sufficiently representative to capture the actual diversity of neurocognition. Even when conducting research within one country such as the US with the purpose of documenting cognitive variation, it is not sufficient to rely on research participants living in more proximity to the universities where the experimental studies take place (Gatzke-Kopp 2016).

Going beyond cultural psychology and neuroscience, there are other methodological approaches with some prospect of chartering human cognitive diversity. One methodological strategy is to explicitly use *non-binary categorizations*, even when focusing on one analytical category such as gender. In addition to employing more than two options, this includes construing categories not in a rigid fashion but instead being open to the possibility of an individual changing from one category to another. A non-binary approach is even needed when dealing with biological sex (Hyde et al. 2019; Massa et al. 2023; Richardson 2022; van Anders et al. 2017). Due to the variety of intersex conditions in humans, various sex-related characteristics (e.g., sex chromosomes, sex hormones, gonads, genitalia, secondary sex characteristics) need not align and do not form distinct sex categories, with Ainsworth (2015) arguing that biological sex should be viewed as forming a spectrum and Richardson (2022) advocating for a 'sex contextualism' that eschews a unique construal of sex across different medical and research contexts.[5] Moreover, researchers have fruitfully used *several analytical categories*, such as employing several construals of 'culture' in their study (Cohen 2009) or using gender, race, ethnicity, and SES (Gatzke-Kopp 2016). Such use of different categories permits representing cognitive variation along several dimensions and capturing the interplay between several features impacting human psychology and mental health. Else-Quest and Hyde (2020) have put forward methodological techniques for how to conduct intersectional analyses as part of quantitative methods in psychology. Likewise, the 'sexual configurations theory' by neuroendocrinologist Sari van Anders (2015) attempts to capture sexual

---

[5] The reader is directed to Kessler's (1990) classical discussion of the treatment of intersex newborns, which reveals two ways in which a sex binary has been constructed (see also Clune-Taylor 2020). There is first a *conceptual* construction of a binary when doctors upon having pondered ambiguous genitalia decide on the child either being a boy or a girl – postulating a binary where it is not present in reality, and sometimes even presenting this assignment to the parents (and themselves) as a medical-scientific finding. Then follows a *causal* construction, where at the time Kessler (1990) wrote, doctors routinely conducted surgery on newborn children – creating a sex binary through human intervention.

orientation, gender, and sexual identity, as well as sexual status in a fashion that permits non-binary and diverse sexualities.

My contrast between approaches that primarily aim at finding sex or gender *differences* in cognition and approaches that are more open to studying cognitive *diversity* is admittedly schematic, but it does give a sense of how *more fruitful* methodologies look like. In contrast to merely searching for statistically significant differences between two groups (e.g., women and men), research attempting to investigate cognitive diversity *uncovers the actual range and shape* of human neurocognition, including data about various cognitive traits that don't exhibit clear between-group differences. And when analyzing and representing findings, such an approach documents variation, including *variation within an analytical category* such as 'female' or 'male.' Such a research orientation is preferable to a sex-difference approach that is restricted to representing the average or median trait within such a category (while contrasting the average for women with the average for men). This methodological superiority also holds compared to the largely outdated research on cognitive differences between the races or any other approach that is merely after cognitive differences between groups. Diversity research using more than one analytical category (such as gender) also has the additional methodological benefit of finding out and describing how human cognition varies *along several dimensions*. Finally, analyzing *complex trait distributions* across various neurocognitive variables fruitfully documents how frequent various combinations of different neurophysiological and cognitive traits are within human populations, even in cases where this cannot be aligned with standard analytical categories. (Beyond representing diversity, decisive advantages of approaches that aim to understand human cognitive diversity will be laid out in the context of explaining diversity in Section 3.2.)

2.3 Why Capturing Cognitive Diversity Matters to Society

So far my discussion has documented the *epistemic* benefits of research agendas that are after human cognitive diversity and use methodologies to investigate and represent such diversity – while contrasting this with the epistemic inadequacies of accounts that are solely interested in uncovering sex differences in cognition and that analyze and represent findings using a typological framework. But now I need to turn to the at least as important *societal* merits or disadvantages of different kinds of research. There are many popular science and media representations making use of psychological and neuroscientific research. Research on sex or gender differences in cognition obviously attracts attention from the general public and has generated many popular accounts (Brizendine 2006, 2010; Gurian and Stevens 2005; Sax 2017; The Gurian Institute et al. 2009). One problem with representations that depict kinds of people using a typological approach (e.g., proclaiming 'the female brain' or 'the female mind') is that they promote stereotypes about groups of people – stereotypes whose omnipresence may well have harmful social effects. This is not only an issue for popular science writers turning complex cognitive science into stereotypical visions about people's cognitive and behavioural attitudes. Scientists may also fail to guard against their research being misrepresented and even actively promote detrimental visions. A case in point is Simon Baron-Cohen (2003), who defends his published work by pointing out that "looking for sex differences is not the same as stereotyping" (p.8), where he characterizes stereotyping as inadequately "reduc[ing] individuals to an average" (p.9). But as we have seen in Section 2.1, even though he occasionally mentions that he is merely representing averages (so that not every woman has a female brain), he predominantly and continually talks in a stereotypical fashion about 'the' female brain and 'the' male brain, or about the female brain type and the male brain type. Adding that the female brain type is about empathizing while the male type is systematizing only exacerbates his stereotypical rendering of groups of people.

As such, stereotypical representations of people draw somewhat simplistic boundaries between kinds of people in terms of their behavioural attitudes and cognitive capacities. But this becomes particularly damaging when some psychological properties (ascribed stereotypically) also have a *social valence* in that they are preferred by society in general or at least are preferred in settings that are socially or economically important. We saw that brain organization theory invokes spatial reasoning, mathematical abilities, nurturing behaviour, and verbal fluency (Section 2.1). Even though all of them can be deemed to be beneficial in some social context, the spatial and mathematical reasoning abilities that brain organization theory attributes to men – in fact confers to men, given the stereotypical and empirically dubious account – are associated with more privileged professions in most societies, while the nurturing skills and more frequent verbal interactions ascribed to women matter to less valued social roles. The situation that also a sexual orientation of being attracted to the other sex is attributed to women and men also reinforces harmful heteronormative stereotypes in any society that harbours people with homophobic attitudes. These societal implications of (dubious) scientific representations are not restricted to issues related to sex and gender – on which I merely focus because they are still subject to active ongoing research. There have been longstanding problems with (pseudo)scientific accounts regarding racial differences regarding behavioural tendencies and cognitive capacities (Gould 1996).[6] Martínez Mateo et al. (2013) also point to colonial value schemes that can be prompted by cultural psychology research contrasting Westerners and other groups of people when the former's psychological tendencies are interpreted from a Eurocentric perspective. Finally, a typological approach used by scientific as well as popular representations is not merely a descriptively inferior scheme but can also create *normative* expectations, where deviations from an alleged type is deemed to be unusual so as to create the impression that conformity to the cognitive or behavioural type is socially expected. As Section 3.3 will discuss in more detail, such normative visions can be reinforced by evolutionary psychology accounts that view some type as being an evolutionary adaptation as well as simplistic developmental accounts that only recognize dimorphic, binary developmental trajectories.

A common objection that attempts to brush away such concerns as mine is that they stem from a *political* agenda, which should not matter for science. This often frames the alternative scientific vision as being the *objective* approach, albeit uncovering socially inconvenient truths (Lloyd 1995). Yet this framing obscures not only that scientists and others promoting alleged scientific results may fail to meet objectivity by endorsing epistemically inadequate views, but also that scientists may disseminate such views for political or other practical purposes – as Section 3.3 will document. The dichotomous framing between political and objective is also inadequate as the use of social-political and other non-epistemic values in science can be perfectly legitimate and conducive to science objectivity (Douglas 2009; Wylie and Hankinson Nelson 2007). By now there is a substantial body of literature on science and values in the larger domain of philosophy of science, which demonstrates not only that the use of environmental, social, and other non-epistemic values by scientists can not only be legitimate, but that this value use can be obligatory in certain contexts (Brigandt 2022a). For an accessible and engaging overview of these issues, the reader is directed to Kevin Elliott's short book *A Tapestry of Values* (2017) or his Cambridge Element *Values in Science* (2022). In a nutshell, scientists have moral responsibility for the foreseeable consequences of their actions as every person does (Douglas 2009). Acting on a scientific account that later turns out to be empirically inadequate can have harmful practical consequences on for

---

[6] While contemporary science eschews the study of cognitive differences between the races, the so-called 'Human Biodiversity Institute' is a group of journalists and fringe scientists who deploy alleged scientific ideas to further a White supremacist political agenda. One particularly subversive aspect of this is their use of the euphemism 'human biodiversity' (Panofsky et al. 2021), while actually denoting an idea that is the very opposite of the notion of human diversity that I advocate to be investigated and valued.

instance the environment or human health. So scientists need to take these potential consequences – and thus the relevant environmental or social values that entail their severity – into account when scientifically attempting to minimize the possibility of their scientific accounts being empirically inadequate (e.g., by demanding more evidence before endorsing some hypothesis). Although this shows that scientists themselves should use non-epistemic in addition to epistemic values, this does not mean that scientists can unilaterally choose which environmental or social values to use. Instead, often the perspectives of societal stakeholders affected by the scientific knowledge in question have to be taken into account (Brown 2020; de Melo-Martín and Intemann 2018; Elliott 2017, ch.7).

Focusing on gender and other human diversity considerations, this Cambridge Element moves within the recent trend of *socially relevant philosophy of science* (Fehr and Plaisance 2010; Plaisance and Elliott 2021). But although the science and values literature has substantially grown during the last two decades, well beforehand there have been critical discussions at the intersection of science and gender, among other things in feminist scholarship (Bleier 1984; Fausto-Sterling 1992; Longino 1990). It also deserves to be emphasized that some of these critical perspectives were not raised from outside of science, but developed by behavioural scientists themselves (Schiebinger 1999). Another important aspect of such critical discussions is that they engage in a joint epistemic and social critique, combining empirical considerations with social-political concerns to reveal better and worse ways to conduct and disseminate cognitive science research (Bluhm 2012, 2020; Fine 2010, 2017; Kourany 2010).

Dubbed the 'aims approach' by Kristen Intemann (2015), one perspective argues that one important way in which environmental, social, and other non-epistemic values can play a legitimate role in science is if such a value promotes the (democratically or otherwise legitimized) aims of a specific case of research (Brigandt 2015b, 2022b; Elliott and McKaughan 2014; Kourany 2010). A benefit of this perspective is that it makes room for values, including non-epistemic values, during *all* stages of research. It is uncontroversial that a scientist is free to choose an ecology research project because of their environmental values (while one could still assume that when then carrying out their research no values may be used). However, the aims approach shows how values matter for all stages of research, given that the aims of a particular research project influence all aspects of it (Brigandt 2015b).

The aims of a particular instance of research clearly guide what *methodologies* are to be employed. The specific aims pursued also impact what definitions and *analytical categories* are to be used – which plays a role from study design to data analysis and the presentation of results. For instance, when classifying personality traits as 'masculine' and 'feminine,' it is inadequate to construe these two categories such that a trait deemed masculine could never also be feminine, that every trait must fall into one of these two categories, or that some traits are more appropriate to some gender (Anderson 1995). Instead, better analytical categories are to be employed, ideally yielding non-sexist research (Eichler 1988). Likewise, when developing a climate change mitigation model that attempts to find the course of action that maximizes global wealth, a definition as *average* wealth across the globe is unable to capture inequities between wealthy and poor countries that may even be enhanced by climate change and/or mitigation strategies (Schienke et al. 2011). Thus, if the aims of research include reducing or at least not exacerbating global inequities, then a measure of wealth is needed that captures the distribution of wealth. A construal of 'wealth' to be safeguarded also needs to consider whether the presence of Indigenous people's hunting, fishing, and other traditional subsistence grounds is to be included – or whether the situation of Indigenous people obtaining food in a novel fashion is equally acceptable (Intemann 2015).

The question of which categories to use as part of climate change models also shows that the aims of research guide what model is to be developed and employed (Potochnik 2012). There are well-known trade-offs where a model cannot properly capture everything, in which case the researchers face a choice of what aspect of reality is most important to represent by this model – based on what the research aims at. For example, general circulation models properly predict basic climate change trends on a global scale, but they cannot capture features in a sufficiently fine-grained manner to provide insight into local trends, in which case regional climate models, which cannot be unified into a global model, are instead to be used (Intemann 2015). When the scientific aim is to intervene in nature or society for practical purposes – be it to conserve species, to ensure that people across the globe get through climate change, or to improve mental health in a country – only a model that serves this aim by capturing relevant causal features will count as an adequate model. In this fashion, values can legitimately influence the considerations that make a model or scientific representation scientifically adequate. Overall, the issue is not whether values are used within science, but whether these epistemic and/ or non-epistemic values promote the specific aims of some research and whether the values are legitimate, for example, answering to the needs of people particularly affected by this research.

In summary, here is why the pursuit of research methodologies that capture cognitive diversity also matters to society. We have seen that methodologies that do not investigate the scope of cognitive variation and use typological representations – for example, proclaiming the female mind or the female brain type – promote stereotypical visions about a group of people. And merely acknowledging cognitive variation within such a group still fails to uncover and describe the cognitive variation to the public. Stereotypes are not only empirically inadequate but can also have a negative societal impact. For instance, portrayals of psychological and affective traits that are too simplistic cannot undergird effective public health initiatives or individual treatment practices that attempt to improve mental health in a society with diverse psychologies and complex psychiatric profiles. Stereotyping is particularly harmful when the cognitive capacity or behavioural tendency ascribed to a group of people is disvalued or disfavoured by society, for example, by being associated with disadvantaged professions or social roles. This undermines the important political aim of achieving equity or at least not exacerbating social inequities.

Not only can some societal ideologies impact scientific research in a problematic fashion, for example, in a patriarchal society it is more natural to investigate sex differences in cognition, but legitimate social values and aims may also inform research agendas. Consequently, in addition to the epistemic benefits of researching cognitive diversity, the *political aim of social equity* (including reducing inequities in the distribution of mental health conditions) calls for avoiding research that emboldens social stereotypes – to the extent to which they are not empirically founded – and concomitantly calls for fostering methodological approaches that are after investigating and representing human cognitive diversity. Beyond capturing the cognitive variation within one analytical category (such as gender), this also calls for methodologies that uncover and describe cognitive diversity regarding several analytical categories, so as to capture that human cognitive variation occurs among different dimensions. In addition to its epistemic benefits, such research would also show that there is no single classification scheme – be it sex, be it race – that science and society could rely upon to capture all the ways in which persons differ in their neurophysiological, cognitive, and behavioural features. Since various methodological approaches are currently present in the cognitive and behavioural sciences, some of which aim primarily at scientifically depicting difference while others are more fruitful for capturing genuine diversity, the normative implication is to support more of the latter.

After this discussion focusing on representing cognitive diversity, Section 3 turns to explaining cognitive diversity. In this context, we will encounter additional reasons why understanding human cognitive diversity also matters to society (Section 3.3).

3 Explaining Human Cognitive Diversity

Section 2 covered different methodological approaches to investigating and scientifically representing human cognitive variation. I schematically but at the same time critically contrasted methodological agendas that primarily aim at finding cognitive differences between women and men with various methodological approaches that pursue strategies for investigating and representing cognitive and behavioural diversity (e.g., by also documenting variation within any one analytical category, capturing variation along several dimensions, or capturing complex distributions of individual cognitive traits). No matter how limited or thorough scientific representations of human cognitive variation may be, there is the further question of what *explains* the origination, current presence, and change of patterns of cognitive variation. Different explanatory agendas and frameworks will be the topic of this section.

Whereas nowadays the study of cognitive differences between races is seen as scientifically unfounded, Section 2 indicated that cognitive differences between women and men is a relatively active area of research, presumably because researchers assume that there are genuine biological differences between the sexes. It is one thing to explain human variation based on the interaction of biological and other factors, but another to pursue explanatory frameworks that presume that cognitive differences between women and men are largely rooted in biology and to disregard the particular role of a person's social environment and their past experiences and behaviour. By contrasting research that effectively operates with a nature-nurture dichotomy (and focuses on explanations in terms of nature) with various alternative explanatory agendas and frameworks, we will see what the epistemic benefits of the latter are. Finally, Section 3.3 discusses why this also matters to society, in particular in the light of the pursuit of social equity.

3.1 Research Operating with a Nature-Nurture Dichotomy

Brain organization theory, as discussed in Section 2.1, views several cognitive traits, including spatial reasoning, mathematical abilities, verbal fluency, and nurturing behaviours, to show some correlation in men (some being a heightened ability and others a reduced capacity) and another correlation characteristic of women. Also called the organization-activational hypothesis, this (alleged) difference is deemed to have a specific biological explanation: due to genetic differences, different levels of sex hormones prenatally organize the brains of female and male fetuses differentially, and upon puberty, sex hormones activate such brain regions in a sex-specific way. Neuropsychiatrist Loann Brizendine (2006) dubs this hormone-based prenatal dimorphic development the 'fetal fork.' Not only the presence of a female and a male package deal of cognitive traits but also the explanatory hypothesis in terms of underlying hormones is dubious.[7] However, my central topic is not *empirical* claims about human cognition, but *methodological* orientations, including the explanatory frameworks that are sought after or used to make sense of findings. Methodologies matter because they guide the trajectory of *future* research. And since it has implications for future research, the adoption of a methodological strategy (e.g., molecular-reductionistic research) or an explanatory vision (e.g., a biological explanation in terms of sex differences) always goes beyond what has been empirically established. Such methodologies can be adopted even when on the empirical level one acknowledges that not every explanation is reductive or that in reality there is no strict nature-nurture dichotomy. In what follows, I take a look at research that aims to find sex differences in cognition and therefore focuses on explanations in terms of biological factors. We will encounter several explanatory biases that can stem from such methodological orientations.

Even without making any explanatory commitment to specific biological features (e.g., sex hormones), researchers may focus on explanations of cognitive variation in terms of biological (rather than social-environmental) factors. When outlining that women "have a small but distinct empathy advantage, a phenomenon buttressed by their biology, assisted by their environment, and made plain by their career moves," psychologist Susan Pinker (2008, 95) assumes an explanatory asymmetry between nature and nurture, where the latter merely has a secondary, auxiliary role (while also reinforcing the cognitive differences previously laid down by nature rather than remodelling the situation). Whereas in Section 3.2 we will encounter alternative explanatory frameworks that envision a thorough interplay between more biological and more social factors, Pinker's taking biology to play a stronger explanatory role than the environment echoes traditional discussions on nature as opposed to nurture, which assume that only one of these prongs could be significant (Brigandt 2024b; Pinker 2002). Similarly, Brizendine (2006, 132) argues that the explanatory landscape should shift from social to biological factors: "While psychologists have emphasized cultural and social explanations for this 'depression gender gap,' more and more neuroscientists are finding that

---

[7] Reviewing the empirical literature, including research on persons with intersex conditions – who due to divergent sex hormone levels or unusual insensitivity to hormones are invoked as naturally occurring experiments – Jordan-Young (2010, ch.7) argues that the overall evidence does not support an explanation focusing on sex hormones. Although the presence of intersex conditions is an instance of human diversity that shows the sex binary to be false (Ainsworth 2015; Clune-Taylor 2020), using intersex persons merely to bolster the largely binary model of the male brain and the female brain does not do justice to human biological and cognitive diversity.

sensitivity to fear, stress, genes, estrogen, progesterone, and innate brain biology play important roles."

When claiming that the 'fetal fork' (consisting in differential hormone exposures) "defines our innate biological destiny," Brizendine (2006, 14) employs the notion of *innateness*. While it is popular to claim some cognitive features to be 'innate,' this notion is scientifically flawed.[8] As Paul Griffiths (2002) has ably argued, the notion of innateness conflates three individually legitimate but completely different properties, so as to prompt fallacies: (1) a trait being monomorphic, that is, universal, within a species, (2) a trait being an evolutionary adaptation, and (3) a trait being rigid in its development, that is, unlikely to change under environmental change. Griffiths adduces several examples and reasons why these three properties can routinely come apart. Here I mention only one, as it is particularly relevant to our topic of explanation: A trait being an evolutionary adaption does not mean that its development is rigid, because developmental plasticity, the ability to learn, and other means of reacting to one's changing environment can be beneficial and thus an adaptation that was favoured by natural selection. Consequently, adducing an evolutionary psychology explanation of gendered cognition (even when cogent) would not entail that this cognitive trait was developmentally rigid and that therefore social-environmental factors did not matter. Generally, nature-nurture debates fallaciously assume that whenever one of the three types of 'innateness' is present (or absent), the others are as well. But having an explanation for one situation (e.g., an evolutionary account in terms of natural selection account) does not pre-empt an explanation of the other (e.g., an ontogenetic explanation in terms of developmental processes). And regardless of whether a trait is (misleadingly) dubbed 'innate,' its development will always involve the interaction of various factors internal to an organism as well as features of its environment.

For explanatory agendas that seek to understand cognitive differences in terms of biology, while at the same time downplaying the impact of social-environmental factors, the developmental rigidity component of the idea of 'innateness' is the most relevant one. Another way that this perspective is popularly expressed is in terms of a cognitive trait being due to a *genetic program*. As a pop science book boldly puts it: "Advances in brain research and neuroscience, however, have given us evidence that your daughter's brain has its own nature, that it's programmed by genes and evolution to function in a certain way, and that much of this will happen no matter what environmental

---

[8] Accordingly, whereas the notion of innateness was prominent in ethology (behavioural biology) seven decades ago (Brigandt 2005), by now it is no longer used within biology.

influences you bring to bear" (The Gurian Institute et al. 2009, 7–8). However, the notion of a 'genetic program' is just like the idea of 'genetic information' for a phenotypic trait not used in contemporary molecular biology, and exhibits several serious flaws (Griffiths 2001; Robert 2004, ch.3).

First, at least when combined with the idea that some genetic program or information for a phenotypic outcome is there because of natural selection, these notions can prompt a teleological interpretation, which takes the 'programmed' phenotypic outcome as the one that is *meant* to be produced – even in cases where another outcome manifests. As Griffiths (2001, 396) puts it: "A 'gay gene' is an instruction to be gay even when the person carrying it is straight." A teleological interpretation views the allegedly 'programmed' phenotype as the normal one and then tends to view divergence from this expectation to amount to some deviation or aberration. Second, the labels 'genetic program' and 'genetic information' falsely maintain that the explanation of a trait's development is only in terms of genes. Yet all cells of an organism contain the same set of genes, so the explanation of development, including the formation of different cell types and tissues must involve something else. One explanatory component is the interaction of genes and other molecular entities inside the cell, which activate, select, and modify the merely potential information contained in genes (Stotz 2006). And interactions between cells and between an organism and its environment matter for the development of any particular trait. Not only cognitive traits but even the very formation of some bones is contingent on a developing organism's interactions with its environmental surroundings, for example, the movements of a chicken embryo inside the egg (Müller 2003).

Third and most importantly, appealing to a 'genetic program' creates the illusion of having explained the phenomenon, while actually having adduced none of the biological entities and interactions that mechanistically account for the development of the cognitive trait. Thus, explanatory agendas that view cognitive difference as to a significant degree due to biology while employing the notion of the trait being 'innate' or 'genetically programmed' use notions that are vacuous at least for explanatory purposes. Indeed, to the extent that some cognitive trait is taken to have a strong biological basis in the sense of developing across various social environments, proclaiming the cognitive trait to be 'innate' or 'programmed' fails to lay out the developmental, neurophysiological, and other biological mechanisms that would explain *why* the trait's development is rigid and insensitive to the social environment – as alleged. The same holds for proclaiming a cognitive trait to be 'hard-wired,' for instance, when Simon Baron-Cohen (2003, 1) maintains that while the "female brain is predominantly hard-wired for empathy," the "male brain predominantly hard-wired for understanding and building systems."

A clear expression of adopting a methodological orientation through pursuing an explanatory framework can be found when Baron-Cohen (2003, 11) wonders "whether the differences that have been found between the sexes really can be explained away as a result of socialization, or whether biology plays a significant role too." His assumption that explaining gender differences in cognition and behaviour in terms of social influences would be 'explaining away' such differences and thus not a genuine explanation – unlike an explanation in terms of biological factors – reveals this psychology researcher to operate with a strong nature-nurture dichotomy that assumes an inherent competition between biological and social explanations. Section 2.1 also documented that Baron-Cohen adopts a typological approach by representing cognitive variation in terms of a female brain type and a male brain type. My discussion explained how Sober (1980) analyzes typological thinking (about biological species) as the adoption of a natural state model, which views the type as forming a natural state, while construing any divergence from the type as a deviation due to some intervening forces. This points to a way in which a typological approach and a nature-nurture dichotomy can reinforce each other, when the female and the male brain types are seen as given by nature (and subject to a genuine explanation) whereas individual variations from a type are seen as mere deviations due to the nurture (and not of explanatory importance).

A more subtle way of methodologically operating with some nature-nurture dichotomy is to assume that both could be separated, in which case it would be possible to study biological influences without studying social influences. An example of this perspective is McCarthy et al. (2017, 471), when these neuroscientists acknowledge that there is a social influence ("the confound of gender") that makes it difficult to "isolate a purely biological contribution to sex differences in human brain and behaviour," while still pursuing the agenda to uncover such a biological contribution. This erroneously presupposes that there is a stratum of purely biological features that is unaffected by a person's experiences, their behaviour, and their environment (which then could be uncovered by an approach studying only 'the biological contribution') and that subsequently social-environmental factors / 'nurture' build on the stratum of 'nature' so as to modify it. Section 3.2 will address in more detail why this causal vision is false and what more appropriate explanatory frameworks look like. In a nutshell, McCarthy et al. (2017, 471) not only express their agenda of focusing on (allegedly existing) purely biological features, but also convey that they view social factors as distorting this biological situation ("the confound of gender") – as opposed to acknowledging that social-environmental influences on neurophysiology shape a person's brain and body and therefore can also count as biological and be subject to biological study. Although sex and gender should not be equated, one cannot consider sex (or sex differences) to be purely biological and unaffected by gender-related features – as Section 3.2 will indicate. Finally, even if some researchers deny holding a nature-nurture dichotomy as an empirical tenet (e.g., by acknowledging the presence mutual influence of more biological and more social factors), without actively studying this mutual influence when focusing on biological features this yields a restricted and even misleading explanatory framework.

Apart from the *conceptual* issue of pursuing an explanatory agenda that focuses on biological influences on cognitive differences (and that possibly operates as if a nature-nurture dichotomy was tacitly adopted), there are also methodological biases resulting from the *experimental* tools being used. One example is when researchers primarily rely on rodent models. Although many researchers are aware of the pitfalls of animal models (Nelson 2018), using rodent models of behaviour can promote the assumption that – compared to humans – the social environment does not have a major impact, and thus that behavioural differences are due to 'nature.' However, not only are lab animals genetically standardized strains that exhibit significantly less genetic diversity than natural populations, their lab environment is likewise controlled, so as to mask the ecological diversity and behavioural complexity (including the organism-social environment interactions) present in natural populations.

In the case of humans, the prominence of brain imaging as an experimental tool can likewise prompt the interpretation that gender differences in cognition revealed by brain scans are due to nature, not nurture. After all, these differences are inside the brain: "Researchers [using MRI] have literally seen what we have always known. There are fundamental gender differences and they start in the very structure of the human brain" (The Gurian Institute et al. 2009, 4). However, the impact of socialization on human cognition must somehow show up in neurophysiology and other bodily processes, so that brain imaging data may well be the result of 'nurture.' While the false interpretation that brain imaging studies reveal cognitive differences that are 'innate' is particularly common among the public encountering neuroscience study depictions in the popular press, even some researchers can fall prey to this misinterpretation. Because of this, Ginger Hoffman (2012) argues that brain imaging studies do not provide evidence for cognitive differences being permanent, hardwired, or innate. She also points out that neurophysiological differences documented by brain scans are not evidence for *psychological* differences between the genders – as some assume – since identical psychological processes may be realized by different neurophysiological processes in different persons. This is a point that we already encountered in the context of cultural neuroscience. Not only is cultural neuroscience open to some of the neurological and neurophysiological variation across cultures being due to socialization, but some of the examples I mentioned in Section 2.2 include how people from different cultures use different neurophysiological processes and even different brain regions for the same psychological task.

So far I have discussed how agendas interested in revealing sex differences in cognition often adopt an explanatory framework that privileges more biological factors over social-environmental factors or operate with a nature-nurture dichotomy that assumes that one could study the explanatory role of purely biological features without taking into account social-environmental features. Now we turn to approaches that explain cognitive diversity in terms of the interplay of various factors, including a person's behaviour and their social environment.

3.2 How to Properly Explain Cognitive Diversity

In Section 3.1, I pointed to some researchers who either empirically assume that gender differences in cognition are largely rooted in 'nature' or simply methodologically set out to focus on the biological contribution to gender differences by studying sex differences in the brain (operating with a nature-nurture dichotomy when assuming that the contributions of nature and nurture could be separated). In either case, we end up with explanatory frameworks that capture (alleged purely) biological factors. This clearly differs from approaches that would also consider the causal role of social-environmental factors and especially those that would capture the causal *interaction* of more biological and more social features. I now turn to such approaches, which by taking into account different types of explanatory factors offer a proper explanation of human neurocognitive and behavioural diversity.

Before I get to examples in the domain of neuroscience, it is worthwhile to mention the general phenomenon of *phenotypic plasticity*. Phenotypic plasticity is the ability of an organism to produce several phenotypic outcomes, depending on the particular environment (Brigandt 2015a; Robert 2004; Sultan 2015). Due to an organism's developmental and physiological plasticity, different phenotypes can result from the same genetic constitution. Apart from phenotypic outcomes that gradually differ from each other this also includes distinct morphologies. For example, in insect societies, the cast-specific morphologies (e.g., small workers and soldiers) develop based on the nutrition on which they were reared. And water fleas have a morph without as well as a morph with a helmet-like extension of the head and a longer tail (in the latter case being harder for predators to swallow), depending on whether the individual is in water with chemicals indicating the presence of predators (Whitman and Agrawal 2009). This illustrates that phenotypic plasticity is beneficial for organisms to deal with variable environments. Because of this, phenotypic plasticity is the product of evolution by natural selection. It is actively being investigated by biologists, including evolutionary biologists. The title of Massimo Pigliucci's (2001) book *Phenotypic Plasticity: Beyond Nature and Nurture* highlights how such research fruitfully goes beyond traditional nature-nurture dichotomies. For since phenotypic plasticity is about the impact of the environment on the organism, including the organism's experiences, investigating plasticity is to investigate 'nurture.' At the same time, since phenotypic plasticity is an evolved response and based on an organism's developmental and physiological organization, research on plasticity is equally well about 'nature' – in fact, addressing the interplay between nature and nurture.

One instance of phenotypic plasticity is *neuroplasticity*. It includes the formation of connections between neurons during brain development to subsequent changes in the structure of neural networks and the activity patterns between neurons. Neuroplasticity underlies the formation of memories and learning more generally. A mistaken nature-nurture dichotomy may conceive of 'nature' as a given stratum on which 'nurture' would only subsequently build – when for instance attempting to investigate the (alleged purely) biological contribution to gender differences in cognition. Yet since neuroplasticity occurs from the very formation of brain tissues throughout an individual's life, there is no separate 'nature' unaffected by an organism's external influences (including during prenatal development). Various phenomena connected to neuroplasticity are being investigated in the cognitive sciences (e.g., Quartz 1999), from research on the mechanisms of neuronal positioning and synaptic remodelling to how brain activity changes in response to a person's experience and behaviour and how brain activity connects up with cognitive and affective processes. One example is the work of Michael Anderson (2014) on neural reuse and the interactive brain. Not only can the same neurocognitive function be performed by different parts of the brain in different individuals, but a person's neuronal network can also come to perform a novel function. In neural reuse, a neuronal element originally developed for one purpose is redeployed for other functions. Due to this kind of neuroplasticity, diverse neurocognitive functions – including higher forms of cognition – can be performed based on overlapping, interacting, and flexibly transforming neural networks.

One way in which a person's social environment affects neurophysiology is through *epigenetic* processes. Apart from non-coding RNA, there are two types of epigenetic processes: DNA methylation and histone modification. Such epigenetic modifications do not change the linear DNA sequences and thus do not change the product for which a gene codes. Instead, epigenetic changes influence the activity of a gene inside a cell and thus the quantity of the gene product that is being generated in a specific part of the body. Epigenetic changes in neurons can be specific to certain brain regions, where they influence neuroplasticity and neurophysiological processes (Qureshi and Mehler 2014). Since epigenetic modifications result from influences outside a cell, including an organism's environment, epigenetic processes are one mechanistic intermediary between a person's environment and their bodily neurocognitive processes (Curley et al. 2011; Powledge 2011; Toyokawa et al. 2012; Tramacere and Bickle 2024). Such research has led to the field of behavioural epigenetics, which includes experimental studies in non-human mammals (Lester et al. 2011). In the case of humans, research on epigenetics investigates not only cognitive processes but also phenomena of relevance to psychiatry, including how social conditions create risk factors for psychiatric symptoms through epigenetic processes (McGowan et al. 2014; Toyokawa et al. 2012; Uddin et al. 2014). One example is research on major psychotic disorders, that is, bipolar disorder and schizophrenia, that includes how social conditions across an individual's lifetime (childhood abuse, chronic stress, and moving to an urban centre or new country) can impact mental health via epigenetic changes (Read et al. 2009; Rutten and Mill 2009).

Even when focusing on phenomena of psychiatric relevance, such research investigating the plasticity-mediated interplay of a person's neurophysiological (and other internal) traits and their social-environmental condition still bears on explaining cognitive diversity, as the variation in social situations across persons, social groups, and societies is one factor generating the prevalence of and *variation* in neurocognitive profiles seen in psychiatric epidemiology. There are also various studies of cognitive plasticity without a focus on molecular epigenetics or neurophysiology. One example from clinical psychology is the 'biological sensitivity to context' theory of Ellis and Boyce (2008), which is broadly similar to the 'differential susceptibility' theory of Jay Belsky (Ellis et al. 2011). Prior models were of course aware that some children are more vulnerable than others in adverse social environments, but for both groups of persons assumed the *same* behavioural outcome in a supportive environment. In contrast, the 'biological sensitivity to context' theory maintains that children who show more clinical symptoms in an adverse environment will however show *superior* behavioural outcomes in a supportive environment. Ellis and Boyce (2008) illustrate this with the label 'dandelion' children and 'orchid' children, where the former show largely the same outcome across different environments, while the latter exhibit higher cognitive plasticity. This approach investigates between-person variation in psychological vulnerability – as a cognitive disposition to respond to social environments – as well as variation in cognitive outcomes.

In psychology, there have been longstanding traditions addressing cognitive plasticity by investigating the causal impact of a person's social environment and their experiences on cognitive development and learning (e.g., Tomasello 2019). Against the idea that intelligence is largely hereditary, psychologists such as James Flynn (2007) and Richard Nisbett (2009) have emphasized the influence of social and cultural contexts on intelligence, including how intelligence has gone up within one society over the decades, among other things due to improvements in educational practices. Socio-economic status is one of the genuinely social features whose causal impact on neurocognitive development has been extensively studied (Tooley et al. 2021; Ursache and Noble 2016). Also addressing the variation of social contexts across societies and cultures, explanatory frameworks in cultural neuroscience address the interplay between internal bodily phenomena (e.g., neurostructural and neurophysiological features) and external socio-environmental processes, including a person's behaviour and experiences (Kim and Sasaki 2014; Kitayama and Park 2010). Such approaches are particularly important for explaining human cognitive *diversity* because they provide tools to account for why cognitive variation between individuals obtains, while instead of privileging one type of explanatory factor they adduce a diversity of causal factors – internal and external to individuals. Such explanations in terms of a complex interaction between many causal factors provide a deeper understanding of the generation and modification of human cognitive diversity.

A clear indicator of scientifically conceptualizing the interplay of biological and social factors is the use of the terms 'sex/gender' or 'gender/sex' by researchers in the cognitive, behavioural, and medical sciences, often researchers working with a feminist perspective (Fausto-Sterling 2012; Jordan-Young and Rumiati 2012; Kaiser et al. 2009). While there are contexts where it is relevant to distinguish sex as a more biological phenomenon and gender as a more social phenomenon, the motivation for using the concept sex/gender is to address contexts where the two cannot be neatly separated, on the grounds of mutual influences between sex and gender as part of the more general interplay of bodily and social-environmental features (Shattuck-Heidorn and Richardson 2019; Springer et al. 2012). In this literature, a few researchers prefer the term 'gender/sex' over the more common 'sex/gender' in an attempt to avoid the interpretation that biological sex would be causally primary or conceptually privileged (Hyde et al. 2019; van Anders et al. 2017). In addition to addressing the entwinement of nature and nurture – including how this interaction explains the generation and modulation of human diversity – such researchers may also eschew the assumption that sex or gender (or sex/gender) would be binary (Hyde et al. 2019; Massa et al. 2023; Richardson 2022; van Anders et al. 2017). The sexual configurations theory by social neuroendocrinologist Sari van Anders (2015) encompasses sexual orientation, gender and sexual identity, as well as sexual status, so as to provide a conceptual framework for cognitive and behavioural research that can scientifically capture non-binary and diverse sexualities.[9] Although as a neuroendocrinologist researching the role of androgens and estrogens on human neurophysiology and behaviour, unlike proponents of brain organization theory who view sex hormones as linear drivers of sexual differentiation in the brain (from sex to gendered neurocognition), van Anders investigates how an adult's behaviour or personal social situation can causally change their sex hormone levels with an impact on neurophysiology (van Anders et al. 2015). She also replaces the traditional association of high levels of testosterone (as seen in males) with aggression and mating and low levels of testosterone (as seen in females) with parenting in favour of a different explanatory model of the causal role of hormones on behaviour (van Anders 2013).

In the context of cultural psychology, Section 2.2 covered the work by Joseph Henrich on the psychology of WEIRD people, that is, persons in Western, educated, industrialized, rich, and democratic societies. Although traditional psychological studies focused on participants from such populations and therefore often considered this psychology (among other things characterized by being individualistic, nonconformist, trusting of strangers, and analytical) to be largely universal, the WEIRD psychology is actually a global minority. Apart from documenting global variation in human cognition, Henrich (2020) has an explanatory account of its historical change, in particular how the WEIRD psychology originated in the first place. While previous accounts of how the economically prosperous and democratic societies of Western Europe arose have focused on changes in economic and other sociological conditions, Henrich's tenet is that we also need to attend to changes in human cognition. In a nutshell, Henrich (2020) points to what he dubs the Catholic church's 'marriage and family program,' which took shape over several centuries and included the prohibition of marriage to close relatives, the discouragement of arranged marriages, the encouragement for newlyweds to set up their independent household, and the creation of spiritual kinship through godparents. Such policies came to transform and undermine the social practices and institutions

---

[9] There are also neuroqueer approaches that do not take a person's sexual orientation to be biologically fixed, but subject to some plasticity during a person's lifetime (Dussauge and Kaiser 2012; Walker 2021a).

hitherto based on tight-knit kinship. Eventually, the new practices also led to a modified psychology, a proto-WEIRD psychology. This furthered certain social and economic developments, which in turn helped the formation of a WEIRD psychology.

Since the marriage and family program had an early effect in some places but was adopted much later in other regions of Western and Eastern Europe, among the various lines of evidence that Henrich adduces is a correlation between the duration of the overall exposure to the new social regime and the current intensity of psychological attitudes characteristic of a WEIRD psychology. Although the Catholic church's marriage and family program obviously has not been in effect in China, across different regions in China, Henrich points to a similar correlation between human psychology and reduced kinship-based practices resulting from local conditions. This also shows that quite unlike contrasting Westerners and Easterners, Henrich is mindful of cognitive variation within a continent and even within a country. Although viewing the church's marriage and family program as the prime driver is empirically debatable, the reason I highlight Henrich's (2020) account is as an instance of an explanatory framework that addresses the mutual interplay of social and psychological changes, which through ongoing feedback creates a *historical change* of human psychology generating cognitive diversity.

So far my discussion has largely focused on developmental explanations (broadly construed), addressing mechanisms operating during the lifetime of an individual, with the potential to generate cognitive diversity across persons. But there are also evolutionary explanations of cognitive diversity. As mentioned in Section 2.1, evolutionary psychology tends to endorse the vision of the 'monomorphic mind,' thereby denying the presence of significant cognitive variation, based on the idea that natural selection would have produced the one optimal cognitive architecture.[10] In contrast, proper evolutionary biology emphasizes variation, as phenotypic variation is required for natural selection to lead to evolutionary change. Genetic variation is the basis of some of the variations in cognition and behaviour we see (Brown et al. 2011). Despite the problematic tradition of proclaiming genetically based cognitive differences between groups, acknowledging a role for genetics is compatible with a human cognitive diversity perspective as the genetic variation does not distinguish human groups but instead is gradual and present within groups. Natural selection need not

---

[10] Evolutionary psychologists rarely have any biological training and lack an understanding of evolutionary biology. This results in accounts of the evolution of human cognition that fall short of the evidential and methodological standards prevailing in evolutionary biology (Buller 2005, 2006; Richardson 2007; Vickers and Kitcher 2003). Although there are feminist approaches in evolutionary psychology, these are wanting as well (Weaver 2017).

favour one type of cognition or behaviour as the optimal one, but can result in diverse behaviour patterns that are maintained within populations, such as the existence of several evolutionarily stable behavioural strategies (Smith 2011). Evolutionary processes can also generate diversity regarding gender-related behaviours in humans and non-human animals, for example, sunfish females have one gender but males can be one of three genders (Roughgarden 2004). Since adjusting one's behaviour to a particular environmental condition, including one's social situation, is adaptive, natural selection can promote phenotypic plasticity, including neuroplasticity, increasing again the spectrum of human cognitive diversity.[11]

In addition to genetic variation and transmission creating diversity, social and other kinds of non-genetic transmission can generate diversity in humans and non-human animals. Eric Smith (2011) argues that since human behavioural diversity surpasses the rate of genetic change, cultural and institutional transmission has played a prominent causal role in the evolution of human behavioural diversity. Rather than focusing exclusively on socially transmitted inheritance, some approaches include gene-culture coevolution, which also addresses the interaction between genetic and cultural evolution, possibly taking the role of the environment in modulating behaviour (e.g., due to phenotypic plasticity) into account (Brown et al. 2011). For instance, cultural neuroscience – seeking to account for the generation of human cognitive diversity – can incorporate evolutionary considerations, where Kim and Sasaki (2014) envision an explanatory framework that not only includes gene-environment interactions (i.e., cognitive plasticity), but also gene-culture coevolution.

In evolutionary contexts, the notion of *niche construction* has become prominent. Also including non-human species, niche construction consists in the situation where an organism's activity modifies its environment in an adaptive fashion, where this modified environment also changes the selection pressures, possibly creating an incentive for genetic change so as to speed up evolutionary change (Brown et al. 2011; Gilbert et al. 2015; Sultan 2015). While evolutionary psychologists view the (social) environment as given, with organisms passively adapting to the situation, in niche construction organisms actively modify their environment, where successive generations continually modify the source of selection driving their evolution. In humans, a classical example is how the advent of cattle farming (as an instance of adaptively modifying our environment) and the concomitant increased consumption of milk favoured the spread

---

[11] Phenotypic plasticity can also drive evolutionary change (Gilbert et al. 2015; Palmer 2012). In contrast to the vision that the advent of new genetic variants always precedes phenotypic change, the reverse is possible due to phenotypic plasticity (West-Eberhard 2003).

of mutations that permitted adults to digest lactose, resulting in a physiological innovation (lactose tolerance) within a relatively short time. This is a clear example of a new human behaviour leading to genetic change. In his account of the evolution of human cognition, Kim Sterelny (2012) argues that innovations in social life led to niche construction driving further cognitive evolution. These human innovations involve new means of sharing, transmitting, and elaborating information that generate informationally enriched environments, from cooperative hunting up to apprentice learning models. Zawidzki (2013) builds on this cognitive niche construction vision when suggesting that the cognitive disposition of 'mindshaping' is an aspect of the distinctively human social niche. In addition to reading others' minds (mindreading), a person also shapes their own mind by imitating others (with a child spontaneously overimitating adults even when not conducive to the child's goals), attending to pedagogical instruction, and adopting social roles and ethical norms. Such mindshaping tendencies not only explain cognitive change in human history, but also cognitive diversity across persons, social groups, and cultures. Overall, due to technological, social-behavioural, and institutional innovations, humans have engaged in various instances of niche construction, so we have created and continue to modify our own behavioural and cognitive diversity (Smith 2011).

An evolutionary explanatory framework that foregrounds cognitive plasticity is Allen Buchanan and Rachell Powell's (2018) account of the *evolution of moral reasoning*. They view humans as fully continuous with non-human animals by explaining the evolution of specifically human abilities for moral reasoning. While previous accounts emphasized how social life in small groups of hominins made it necessary to coordinate social cooperation and mitigate non-altruistic behaviour, Buchanan and Powell (2018) argue that such accounts only yield altruistic behaviour within small groups, while having to view between-group attitudes as generally hostile, which is insufficient for explaining modern human moral capacities. From Buchanan and Powell's perspective, an appropriate evolutionary explanation of moral psychology must be able to account for how human societies have come to make the set of persons that they see as deserving moral regard as larger and more inclusive – while also being able to account for morally regressive historical instances where the scope of moral regard was again restricted. This is where cognitive plasticity enters. On their explanatory framework, humans possess plastic moral mechanisms (as evolutionary adaptations), which during an individual's development promote the formation of tribalistic attitudes in response to the perception of threats from outside of one's group, while promoting more urbane or cosmopolitan attitudes if no threats are perceived. These threats can consist in real situations such as a high prevalence of pathogens, which can spread easier across groups that more freely interact with each other, but also in merely perceived threats that have been publicly promoted within one's social community about strangers, including by modern political propaganda. While Buchanan and Powell historically explain how we humans have overall become more and more morally inclusive (due to social reductions in actual and perceived threats), they are also able to capture morally regressive trends, so as to account for some of the cognitive diversity seen across human cultural groups.

I have covered various explanatory approaches that understand human cognition in terms of the interplay of features internal and external to individuals. Compared to explanations in terms of biological sex differences only, accounts in terms of the interaction of neurophysiological and social-environmental features yield much richer explanatory frameworks to account for the presence of human cognitive diversity and the change in the shape of human cognitive variation. Now it is time to address the societal implications of the use of certain explanatory frameworks in cognitive science.

3.3 Why the Explanatory Frameworks Used Matter to Society

My discussion has contrasted approaches that focus on hormonal and other biological causes of gender differences in cognition with approaches that explain cognitive diversity based on various causal factors, including features internal to persons and social-environmental features influencing a person's experiences, behaviour, and cognition. The latter offers richer explanatory frameworks of an individual's cognition and cognitive diversity across persons by not only including more causal factors, but also by explaining in terms of the *interaction* of various factors, internal as well as external to individuals. Beyond the epistemic advantages of explanatory frameworks that account for cognitive variation based on the interplay of neurophysiological and social-environmental processes, there are also social-political reasons for fostering such approaches. Section 2.3 already argued that research using a typological approach to represent sex or gender differences in cognition (e.g., portraying 'the' male mind and 'the' female mind) reinforces stereotypes about groups of humans, which have harmful social consequences when stereotypic cognitive abilities have a social valence where some abilities are preferred within a society while others are disvalued, making a group of persons cognitively inferior compared to another one. In the present context of explanatory frameworks, this situation is exacerbated by accounts exclusively focusing on genetic, hormonal, or other biological causes of sex and gender differences in cognition, as among the public this makes these differences seem natural and hard to change, so as to disincentivize social efforts of reducing inequities.

There is a longstanding history of drawing political implications from claims about group differences being rooted in nature, for example, genetics (Gould 1996; Lewontin et al. 1984). In the case of race, one prominent agenda has been to maintain that educational and other social reforms are moot as cognitive differences between different races (including within one country like the US) are largely genetic (Herrnstein and Murray 1994). While Section 3.2 pointed to explanatory approaches actively investigating different instances of phenotypic plasticity, such arguments claiming IQ differences to be unchangeable by social means are fallacious by ignoring the very phenomenon of phenotypic plasticity. Even if different races were genetically characterized, an IQ difference being present in a present social environment does not tell us anything about whether it would persist, be reduced, or even reversed in a different social environment. More important to my present topic is that such (flawed) empirical claims have repeatedly been used to either explicitly advance social-political tenets or promote such empirical contentions among the public and policy-makers to influence social policy. Apart from race, political implications have repeatedly been drawn from claims about gender differences in cognitive capacities and psychological tendencies being to a substantial extent rooted in biological differences, as Janet Kourany (2010, ch.1) among many others has documented.

In contrast to viewing cognitive diversity as a contingent matter resulting from complex interactions between more biological and more social-environmental facts, claims about biological differences biologize some facts that are social facts, as Choudhury and Kirmayer (2009) point out in the context of cultural neuroscience (also drawing connections to colonial traditions in psychiatry).[12] Jordan-Young (2010, ch.10) makes explicit that because gender and other phenotypic differences are subject to variation across environments, it is circular or teleological to proclaim one single human social environment (e.g., one that exhibits gender differences that one takes to be most pronounced) to the 'natural' or 'ideal' environment. Adaptationist evolutionary stories can exacerbate the normative implications drawn from alleged cognitive or behavioural situations, insofar as the latter are seen as being present for an evolutionary purpose since they are optimal in our human social environment (as far as

---

[12] While Section 3.2 emphasized how social-environmental factors (including based on evolutionary niche construction) generate human cognitive diversity, one should acknowledge that this need not be continuous cognitive variation but can also result in gendered cognition. Indeed, Fine et al. (2017) suggest that it is not genetic inheritance but the inheritance of socio-environmental conditions that creates *stability* of sex-related behaviour across generations (while the *variability* of sex-related behaviour across individuals and generations is due to biological as well as socio-environmental factors). But even in this case, it is important to stress the historical contingency of the various factors involved, to counter the fatalistic visions about gender and other social differences addressed below.

natural selection is concerned). A case in point is claiming the male brain and the female brain to be evolutionary adaptations to two different ecological niches, each of which brain type is alleged (without evidence) one of two possible cognitive optimal strategies to socially interact (Baron-Cohen 2003).

Rather than belabouring the long history of claims about sex differences in cognition, what I want to emphasize is that claims of social-political relevance are still being made based on contemporary research on sex differences in the brain. Neuropsychiatrist Loann Brizendine (2006) directly addresses the infamous contention made by the former president of Harvard University Lawrence Summers about the cognitive root of the gender gap in tenured positions in the STEM fields. While Brizendine does not take there to be a significant difference between boys and girls before puberty, she does endorse implications similar to Summers' when proclaiming there to arise a "difference in their mathematical and scientific capacity" soon after puberty that is due to sex hormones ("as estrogen floods the female brain, females start to focus intensely on their emotions and on communication – talking on the phone and connecting with their girlfriends at the mall. At the same time, as testosterone takes over the male brain …, " p.7). As we have seen, the prominent psychologist Simon Baron-Cohen (2003) postulates a male brain as opposed to a female brain. Although he claims to not assume that every woman has a female brain, at the same time he views each brain type as strongly associated with the respective biological sex, in fact maintaining that sex hormones causally underlie each brain type. He also draws implications of social-political relevance by viewing each sex-based brain type – unlike any other factor – to entail a clear-cut aptitude for different social professions: "People with the female brain make the most wonderful counselors, primary-school teachers, nurses, carers, therapists, social workers, mediators, group facilitators, or personnel staff. … People with the male brain make the most wonderful scientists, engineers, mechanics, technicians, musicians, architects, electricians, plumbers, taxonomists, catalogists, bankers, toolmakers, programmers, or even lawyers" (p.185).

In a possibly bolder fashion, while acknowledging that the gender gap in professions has been reducing in Western countries during the last few decades, psychologist Susan Pinker (2008) contends that there are serious limits to reducing the gender gap further. Considering the contrary assumption that "if the social order had *really* changed, women would be exactly like men by now. They'd make the same choices, opting in equal proportions for chief executive positions, careers in theoretical physics, or political office" (p.10), Pinker takes it to have been disproven by women and men still not making identical choices. Unsurprisingly, her explanation for the gender gap being something that cannot be removed (and in this sense is to be tolerated) is biological: "If boys and girls,

are on average, biologically and developmentally distinct from the start …
wouldn't these differences affect their choices later?" (p.7).

Only some cognitive or behavioural scientists make claims that directly
address issues relevant to social policy, such as gendered aptitude for different
professions. But what ultimately matters is the societal impact of explanatory
frameworks that focus on the biological basis of cognitive differences (without
detailing the role of social-environmental features). These can convey to the
general public as well as policy-makers that cognitive differences are largely
rooted in biology and inaccessible to behavioural or social changes. Ilan Dar-
Nimrod and his colleagues have conducted psychological studies that show that
a person's beliefs about certain traits or situations (e.g., heart disease or obesity)
being genetic and other deterministic assumptions do indeed promote fatalistic
attitudes, which tend to reduce a person's efforts at changing or influencing the
situation (Dar-Nimrod and Heine 2011; Heine 2016; Heine et al. 2017). Not
only can such fatalistic visions impact public policy, but when our attempts at
influencing a situation diminish, this reduction in the socio-environmental
contribution to the overall causal factors influencing a trait within a society
even entails a quantitatively higher genetic contribution to the trait (Kõiv 2023).
In the case of mental disorders, the public tends to have more negative attitudes
towards people with mental health problems if mental illness is perceived to
have genetic-biological causes as opposed to psychosocial causes (Walker and
Read 2002), impacting not only the psychiatric treatment by doctors and nurses
but also how persons with mental health issues are treated within society.

The socio-politically desirable alternative is to foster scientific research that
includes ways in which human behaviour, cognition, and mental health are also
influenced by various social-environmental conditions. Covering more factors
that are under societal control (compared to other explanatory frameworks),
such research can be fruitfully used for public policy purposes. This is particularly important in the case of social inequities regarding psychological abilities
and mental health. In the related context of bodily health, philosopher Jonathan
Kaplan (2010) offers an insightful perspective. Focusing on race-based drugs,
such as the drug BiDil used to remedy heart problems in African Americans, he
argues that even if these drugs work by treating physiological and other bodily
conditions, this does not entail that the condition is genetic. Instead, as an
instance of socio-environmental conditions influencing biological conditions,
racism involves chronic stress that can lead to hypertension and other heart
problems.[13] While highlighting the interplay of biological and social features

---

[13] Environmental racism more generally highlights how social inequities can negatively impact the
health of minorities, also including the Indigenous populations of some countries.

and acknowledging that such health conditions can be treated by drugs or other biomedical means, Kaplan's core point is that the focus ought to be on fighting the racism that creates such health inequities in the first place, and therefore on social factors and changes in social conditions.[14] This also holds for our context of human cognition. Social disparities can among other things be found in the case of psychiatric conditions (including their incidence and severity). And mental health disparities should not only be addressed by pharmacological and other medical means, but also by preventative policies and social reforms that improve mental health within society and reduce mental health inequities.

In summary, research agendas that are after cognitive differences between groups are not only likely to promote stereotypes about groups, but also tend to be interested in the biological basis of such differences. The latter research has the socially problematic effect of making psychological differences seem hard to change and even naturally given. In the context of gender differences in psychology, several have critically addressed how some approaches within cognitive and behavioural science can reinforce the presence of oppressive social conditions, while at the same time pointing to alternative avenues for research that investigate neuroplasticity and how the human social environment influences gendered cognition (Eliot 2009, 2011; Fine 2010; Jordan-Young 2010; Valian 2014). More generally, explanatory frameworks that detail the mutual interaction of neurocognitive and social-environmental processes convey to the public that the present shape of human cognitive diversity is contingent and likely to undergo further change. Moreover, to the extent to which it is socially desirable to influence some aspects of neurophysiology, for example, improving mental health while also reducing social inequities in mental health, scientific explanatory frameworks that include the role of socio-environmental factors are better poised to suggest relevant options for social policy.

4 Neurodiversity, Dysfunction, and Human Nature

While also emphasizing the societal relevance of scientific accounts, my discussion so far has centred on how to *scientifically* represent and explain human cognitive variation. Now it is time to address how *we* should generally understand and appraise cognitive variation. Sections 2 and 3 argued that to properly arrive at an account of cognitive diversity, investigations are needed that come to represent the full range and complexity of cognitive variation (including variation along several dimensions) as well as to uncover the variety of causal factors that explain how the shape of human cognitive variation has been generated (and is

---

[14] Tabery (2023) and Valles (2019, 2021) likewise emphasize the need to attend to the social causes of health disparities.

continuously being transformed). Compared to the neutral term 'variation,' the label 'diversity' has a positive valence. In the discussion so far, I have already used the label human cognitive *diversity* to flag that cognitive diversity is not just a reality, but something that should not be disvalued. This section articulates how and why human cognitive diversity should be appreciated.

I start with biological considerations that prompt us to recognize the diversity of human bodily and cognitive functioning, which resonates with ideas from disability studies and the neurodiversity movement. Then I engage with different positions surrounding human nature. While my previous critical targets were scientific approaches (e.g., research on sex differences in cognition as an impoverished scientific agenda), Section 4.2 turns to a tradition within philosophy as a target: neo-Aristotelian ethics employing the idea of natural goodness as opposed to natural defect. This involves the notion that for any species there is a life-form – a species nature with normative implications – and thus a unique way to exhibit natural goodness and functioning. I will reject these neo-Aristotelian notions as running afoul of human diversity and therefore as fatally flawed. My discussion concludes by addressing implications for the very idea of human nature, including whether we should use the notion of human nature at all, given that it tends to convey a unique set of features characteristic of humans as opposed to substantial diversity.

4.1 Recognizing the Diversity of Bodily and Cognitive Functioning

In addition to contributions by philosophers (e.g., Barnes 2016; Silvers 2003; Tremain 2023), disability studies is an interdisciplinary field. One of the milestones in disability studies scholarship has been to replace the medical model of disability with the social model of disability (Oliver 1990; Wasserman and Aas 2023). The medical model assumes that a disability is a bodily difference (the absence of some organ or the inability to carry out some bodily function), which is present whenever a person exhibits this bodily condition. In contrast, the social model suggests that a disability does not just reside inside one's body; instead, at least some kinds of disabilities depend on and arise from a person's social context. For instance, whereas a person with paralyzed legs will exhibit a disability in a societal context where no wheelchairs are present, in a context where there are plenty of wheelchair ramps, elevators, and similar infrastructural and institutional features, the same person with the same bodily constitution may have a very high mobility. The social model has been criticized by disability scholars as failing to capture all aspects of the lives of disabled persons, including cases where accessibility features and accommodations cannot remove suffering or achieve social participation (Dokumacı 2023). Still, by not misconstruing social barriers as personal bodily or medical barriers, the social model has the important social-political impact of calling for social-institutional changes that serve the needs of as many people as possible. The same holds for cognitive disabilities (Chapman 2023). For some cognitive conditions, such as ADHD, the disability arises not just due to a person's internal neurophysiology, but also in virtue of the performance demands that modern societies (taking neurotypical persons as the standard) impose in the workspace or the learning environment, combined with the absence of accommodations. Again, the social-political impact is to call for social environments that minimize cognitive differences manifesting as disabilities, so as to reduce inequities between persons regarding fully participating in social life.

In line with our topic of human cognitive diversity, of primary interest is the notion of cognitive disability and cognitive dysfunction. A new perspective on this matter is the *neurodiversity* approach, which originated during the last three decades. This approach maintains that neurodiversity, that is, the cognitive diversity across persons, is a natural and even valuable form of human diversity. Not only neurotypical persons but also various neurodivergent persons, such as people with autism, ADHD, dyslexia, Tourette's syndrome, and colour-blindness fall under the umbrella of neurodiversity by simply exhibiting alternative cognitive styles (Brigandt 2024b). When arguing that there is not just one normal or 'right' type of cognitive style – just like there is not one normal gender or race – a neurodiversity perspective comes to see neurominorities as analogous to other minorities (Walker 2021b). Consequently, neurodivergent minds should not be pathologized as having a condition that is conceptualized as to be 'cured.' Originally, the neurodiversity movement gained recognition based on the idea that some neurodivergent brains convey unusual aptitudes and skills. This has been particularly vivid in the case of so-called 'high-functioning' autistics, with Greta Thunberg viewing her Asperger's not as an illness, but as a genuine superpower. This points to conflicting views on the scope and nature of neurodiversity. Whereas some maintain that 'high-functioning' autistics but not 'low-functioning' autistics fall under the neuro-diversity umbrella as instances of normal cognitive variation (e.g., Jaarsma and Welin 2012), others attempt to make room for 'low-functioning' autistics by at least by using a different notion of human flourishing and social functioning for such persons (Doan and Fenton 2013; Fenton and Krahn 2007). As an instance of a bolder version of a neurodiversity paradigm, Nick Walker (2021b) eschews the pathologization of any neurodivergent brain, and views the very notions of 'high-functioning' and 'low-functioning' autism as presupposing the traditional pathology paradigm and its idea of cognitive normalcy that Walker reject.

I will not take a stance on the criteria that could delimit normal cognitive variation from neurocognitive or mental disorder. Instead, my agenda is to emphasize that cognitive diversity is generally to be appreciated and that neurodiversity has a larger scope than typically assumed – especially that diverse ways of cognitive functioning are perfectly possible. To this end, I point to Ron Amundson's (2000) 'Against normal function,' which for me has been one of the most insightful philosophical articles to date. His discussion covers physical as well as cognitive function and dysfunction. In a nutshell, while disability scholars have found the social model of disability a better model for disability than the medical model (without scrutinizing the medical model on empirical grounds), Amundson questions the very biological coherence of the medical model. More precisely, Amundson challenges a biological notion of normalcy as found for instance in Boorse's (1997, 7) biostatistical theory of disease, which construes the normal function of a bodily part or process in terms of what is statistically typical within a "natural class of organisms of uniform functional design." Whereas disability studies scholars have indeed questioned Boorse's "definition of disease *in terms of* biological normality," they "do not challenge the concept of biological normality itself" (Amundson 2000, 35) – which is precisely Amundson's agenda. He appeals to Anita Silvers's (1998) distinction between the *level of performance* of a function and the *mode of performance* to make the point that whereas biological notions of normalcy (at least tacitly) assume that there can only be one normal mode of performance, "diversity of [mode of] function is a fact of biology" (34). And instead of the (one alleged normal) mode of function the focus should be on a person's level of performance.

Amundson (2000) adduces several examples that illustrate diverse modes of functioning, especially atypical modes that are still functional. One basis for this is phenotypic plasticity (see also Brigandt 2015a). In the 1940s, the biologist Slipjer studied a two-legged goat, which was born without forelegs and had learned to walk bipedally. Not only had it acquired a for goats untypical yet functional mode of locomotion, due to phenotypic plasticity it also exhibited several bodily adjustments that were conducive to a bipedal way of life, including an S-shaped spine, an ovally (rather than V-shaped) thorax, and other atypically shaped bones or positioned muscled. Although such an S-shaped spine is well-known from humans and kangaroos as bipedal mammals (and there are further instances of two-legged goats), it is clearly not a species-typical mode of functioning. Amundson also points to surgical transposing of nerve-to-muscle attachments in humans (an intervention in case of some injuries and physical disabilities). Upon an adaptation period, this yields a high level of performance despite the atypical mode of innervation, where nerves have been switched between quite different muscles.

There are also cases of hydrocephaly where the buildup of cerebrospinal fluid in the cranium results in a person having only 10 percent of the statistically typical brain tissue, but where the person is cognitively and functionally undistinguishable from others. Of further interest are ranking schemes for athletes in wheelchair basketball, which assign performance points to individual players to ensure that the two teams on the court are comparable in terms of a team's overall points. As Amundson (2000) explains, original ranking schemes focused on upper-body musculature, but were replaced as they failed to measure an athlete's playing performance. The reason is that different athletes can achieve the same performance in different ways. Apart from upper-body strength, the ability to achieve balance in the lateral plane is one of several factors, so some athletes with below-average muscle function make use of another mode of playing successfully. Finally, signed languages offer a striking example of how diverse and distinct modes of cognitive functioning can be. Sign languages used within deaf communities are grammatically and semantically as complex as other languages. But they do not employ vocal sound and auditory perception as what has often been taken to be 'essential' to a language (based on our evolutionary history), and instead adopt a distinct mode of perception.

Amundson's (2000) criticism addresses not just the assumption that there is one normal mode of function, but also that the *mode* of function of able-bodied persons is taken as the normal one and then imposed upon others even when this results in a decreased *level* of performance (see also Silvers 1998). One example of his is Norman Daniels's (1987) account according to which the primary goal of healthcare is the preservation and restoration of normal functioning, which Daniels construes in terms of the (alleged) species-normal functioning. Amundson also points to rehabilitation programs for children affected by thalidomide in Canada in the 1960s. These children were prohibited from using wheelchairs and instead strapped onto specifically designed platforms that loosely resembled legs. Employing substantial effort, a child could teeter the platform back and forth to slowly move in a mode that vaguely mimicked walking. Another example of his is schools for the deaf that prohibited them from using sign language – similar to how government schools for Native Americans prohibited them from using their Indigenous languages.[15] Based on the doctrine of 'oralism,' these deaf children instead had to learn to lip-read and to speak aloud, which are skills extremely hard to learn even for not profoundly deaf persons and of no use in interactions among deaf people. (And the limited integration with hearing persons could have been equally

---

[15] Residential schools for Indigenous children in Canada practiced the same, among its larger aim of assimilating Indigenous children into European-Canadian culture and eradicating their original identity (for which we now have the term cultural genocide).

well achieved by teaching sign language to hearing children.) Also pertaining to cognitive rather than physical function, Amundson's final case is when educators discouraged autistic children from stimming, so as to behave and look more like neurotypical ('normal') children. Stimming (also called self-stimulatory behaviour) is the use of repetitive bodily movements, such as flicking one's fingers in front of one's eyes. Since standard environments create a sensory overload for many autistic persons, stimming is beneficial as it reduces the perceptual chaos for people with heightened sensory sensitivity and helps them to focus – even if it is a mode of behaviour different from the neurotypical one.[16]

In summary, among the natural variation seen in any species are also diverse modes of functioning. The same level of performance can be achieved by several distinct modes of functioning – physical as well as cognitive functioning. It is therefore empirically futile to adopt a notion of 'normal function' that would presuppose one unique mode of function, such as some species-typical way of being. And adopting the latter approach has routinely privileged the characteristics of able-bodied and neurotypical people, while judging others to be abnormal or defective in some way.

4.2 Against Dysfunction and Defect in Neo-Aristotelian Ethics

The notion of function as opposed to dysfunction / defect also plays a prominent role in a major current philosophical tradition: *neo-Aristotelian virtue ethics*. Neo-Aristotelianism is the dominant approach in contemporary virtue ethics, and I will focus on the strand of the larger neo-Aristotelian tradition relying on the notion of natural goodness, as represented by Philippa Foot (2001), Rosalind Hursthouse (1999), and Michael Thompson (2008). This neo-Aristotelian ethics is often presented as an 'ethical naturalism.' We will soon see that it is anything but a naturalistic approach that would rely on biological or other empirical ideas. Instead, the label 'naturalism' stems from the approach centrally using the idea of *natural goodness* – goodness in nature as it is also found in plants and animals – as opposed to *natural defect*. This natural goodness is specified by the nature (or life-form) of a species. In the case of humans, the account therefore employs the notion of *human nature*, while adopting an essentialist and teleological conception of human nature, with which I will take issue.

Neo-Aristotelian ethics relies on the idea of flourishing, where an organism's flourishing is construed in terms of how well the organism functions as specified

---

[16] Many of you will remember the fidget spinner craze from 2016. Based on the controversial idea that using a fidget spinner helps children especially those with ADHD, many bought a fidget spinner for their children (and even grandchildren). This reveals the double standard that when all the neurotypical kids do it in the classroom it is accepted – whereas analogous behaviour used to be discouraged when performed by autistic children.

by the nature of the species to which it belongs. More specifically, organs and vital activities that function and support the organism's flourishing are instances of natural goodness (otherwise a natural defect). Using an example by Philippa Foot, although not every oak tree may happen to have sturdy roots and a stable trunk, an oak tree *must* have sturdy roots and a stable stem – if this 'natural necessity' is not present, the oak tree is naturally defective. While good for a reed plant, pliability is a defect in an oak tree. The notion of natural goodness likewise applies to animals, for example, "the hearing of a gull that cannot distinguish the cry of its own chick" is a natural defect (Foot 2001, 42). This is a teleological vision that postulates natural norms:

> These 'Aristotelian necessities' depend on what the particular species of plants and animals need … These things together determine *what it is for members of a particular species to be as they should be, and to do that which they should do*. (Foot 2001, 15, emphasis added)

The very point of this ethical naturalism is that the notions of natural goodness and defect also apply to *humans*. To be sure, when it comes to specifically *moral* judgements about a person's actions, the account is more sophisticated than insisting that a woman attend to the cry of her own child (in analogy to a female gull for its chick). In the case of human action, various capacities for rational reasoning, especially practical reasoning and virtuous character, are crucial. Hursthouse (1999, 200–201) distinguishes different ends with respect to which different species are evaluated: "(i) individual survival, (ii) the continuance of the species, and (iii) characteristic pleasure or enjoyment/characteristic freedom from pain. . . . [in] social animals, we find that a fourth end comes in, namely (iv) the good functioning of the social group." The position is not that some behaviour is morally good for humans whenever it is naturally good in a non-human animal. Rather, the tenet is that the concept of 'natural goodness' that we deploy when evaluating plants and non-human animals is the same concept that forms the basis for morally evaluating human action and rational capabilities – so as to ground moral philosophy in features about nature. Immorality is viewed as a natural defect, as a failure of practical rationality.[17]

---

[17] Pioneered by Amartya Sen and Martha Nussbaum, the 'capabilities approach' to human development has Aristotelian roots in the case of Nussbaum's (2000, 2011) version. Unlike normatively evaluating persons in terms of their cognitive and rational capacities (as done by the natural goodness approach), the capabilities approach politically calls for societies to enable and foster various human capacities that are crucial for human flourishing and social justice within societies and around the globe. Crucially, the capacities approach captures cultural and other diversity, as opposed to imposing one standard on everyone. In contrast to John Rawls' account (and the natural goodness account, I add), Nussbaum (2011, 87) does not want to exclude persons with "severe physical and cognitive disabilities" based on their allegedly lacking rationality.

There have been previous criticisms of neo-Aristotelian ethics from naturalistic perspectives informed by biology. Lewens (2010) points out that biological considerations about the function of organismal traits show that a particular trait's contribution (e.g., to survival, reproduction, and other organismal flourishing) is always a matter of degree, which is at odds with Foot singling out some traits that are claimed to be categorically necessary (and considering the absence of this trait to be a categorical defect). Most such criticisms have argued that the notion of function underlying neo-Aristotelian judgements of natural goodness needs to be the etiological concept of a function, that is, function in the sense of selected effect. However, employing this notion of function entails an account of morality that would condone ethically clearly reprehensible behaviour – which is a good reason not to endorse the natural goodness approach. The reductio argument is that human tendencies for aggression, sexual violence, strong in-group cooperation and conformity (even when it has ethically problematic effects), and xenophobic reactions to out-group members have some evolutionary basis involving natural selection (including cultural evolution), and thus would count as functional in the sense of selected effects (Millum 2006; Odenbaugh 2017; Woodcock 2006).

Anticipating this objection, Foot (2001, 32) reacts by eschewing the etiological notion and instead invoking some everyday concept of 'function.' However, not only does she not articulate this use, but she falsely assumes that everyday terms have a single meaning. Even in evolutionary biology, several different notions of function are already used, as pointed out by philosophers (Amundson and Lauder 1994; Wouters 2003). In my view, we need philosophical notions that are articulated together with a defence of why using this notion is appropriate – which involves considerations about the practical consequences of language use among other empirical considerations. As philosophers have made plain under the label of 'conceptual engineering,' attempting to revise and improve concepts as well as discard concepts that are problematic or even socially harmful may involve going beyond ordinary and current uses of a term (Brigandt and Rosario 2020; Burgess et al. 2020; Nado 2021). In contrast, Foot's appeal to some unarticulated notion of function that cannot be scrutinized opens the door to using one's personal and biased judgements about natural goodness.[18]

---

[18] Other proponents of neo-Aristotelian ethics have endorsed Foot's approach: "Foot's view of function is independent of any empirical theory about these matters" (Hacker-Wright 2009, 312). In contrast, Odenbaugh (2017) argues that to arrive at the *normativity* that an ethical theory requires, neo-Aristotelians have to adopt the etiological concept of function – and then are committed to the unacceptable moral judgements entailed.

Beyond these previous criticisms of neo-Aristotelian ethics, I point to a different problem with this approach. In line with my emphasis on cognitive and other diversity, I challenge the neo-Aristotelian idea that there is a *species-wide nature* that can be used to evaluate not only moral action in humans but also cognitive traits in humans and other species. The previously mentioned examples by Philippa Foot (2001, 15) indicate that her vision of "what it is for members of a particular species to be as they should be" assumes that certain species-typical features must be present, otherwise there is a defect. However, we learned from Ron Amundson (2000) that diverse modes of function can all be functional and offer a high level of performance, so one should not insist on only one trait or function and denounce all others as defective or disabled. Scott Woodcock (2006) has previously highlighted the inadequate vision neo-Aristotelianism entails for disabled persons.[19] I will go beyond Woodcock's focus on Foot as the neo-Aristotelian account criticized as well as his scrutiny of various individual examples of alleged natural defects, by challenging the very idea of a species-wide nature that would yield adequate normative judgements (again relying on Amundson's insights). To this end, I first take a look at Michael Thompson's (1995, 2008) notion of the *life-form* of a species, which is an articulation of the idea of a nature that grounds normative judgments of natural goodness and defect. Other proponents of neo-Aristotelian ethics have endorsed Thompson's life-form concept, including Foot: "to understand certain distinctive ways in which we describe individual organisms, we must recognize the logical dependence of these descriptions on the nature of the species to which the individual belongs. Species-dependence is his [Thompson's] leitmotif" (Foot 2001, 27).

Thompson's (2008, 20) starting point are statements like "the domestic cat has four legs" and "bobcats breed in spring" (see also Thompson 1995). He calls them 'natural-historical judgments' or 'natural-teleological judgments,' while making plain that he does not consider them to be either empirical generalizations or empirical statements about a species' natural history in the sense of evolutionary history.[20] Instead, he considers them to express essential

---

[19] Woodcock (2006, 452) considers a potential neo-Aristotelian position on disability and still finds it wanting: "it is not clear that restricting our use of the word 'good' to a narrow form of moral evaluation will eliminate the objectionable implications that follow from Foot's view. . . . 'When I [the neo-Aristotelian] said earlier that you were defective in a normative sense, I meant only to say that humans are creatures who ought to be able-bodied and have the capacity to reproduce in the same way that spiders ought to have eight legs and spin webs. You can still be considered a good person in the specifically moral sense that refers to your voluntary actions . . . ' I [Scott Woodcock], for one, would still be rather uncomfortable explaining this to someone who is disabled or sterile."

[20] "These propositions are in no sense hypotheses about the past." (Thompson 2008, 79)

properties of a species, where he dubs this essential nature of a species its 'life-form.' This life-form grounds teleological and normative judgments about individual members of a species, including judgements about natural goodness and defect. Thompson's striking position is that the notion of a life-form is a precondition for viewing anything as a living thing, and thus prior to empirical statements about living things and in fact presupposed by biological assertions.[21] This anti-naturalistic stance is illustrated by his interpretation of swampman cases. It has been previously debated whether a spontaneously arising creature that happens to be a perfect duplicate of a person would have thoughts and other mental representations (where a teleosemantic account of mental representation would find lacking the history that endows mental symbols with their content). Thompson (2008, 60) is bolder by maintaining that swampman would not be alive and not even have any anatomical structures, on the grounds that a mere physical duplicate does not bear a life-form.

Thompson (2008) is clear that one and the same life-form holds for all members of a biological species. Indeed, although he generally prefers to use his more technical term 'life-form,' he also views it as synonymous with the notion of a species: "*life-form* or *species*" (p.31), "the concept of a life-form or species" (p.48). However, he does not see the need to offer any justification for why a subspecies or other group of individuals could not have its own life-form, and thus why there could not be a diversity of life-forms present within a species such as ours. And despite maintaining that a life-form is uniformly shared across a species, he does not argue for why such a life-form could not actually be shared by a whole taxon above the species level, such as a genus.[22] We have seen that neo-Aristotelian approaches to ethics relying on the notion of natural goodness adopt the idea of Aristotelian natural necessities. This is an organ, a vital activity, a behaviour, or a cognitive capacity that ought to be present; and a natural defect is claimed to be present whenever an individual does not have this specific feature. Such a normative judgement about an individual depends "on the nature of the species to which the individual belongs" (Foot 2001, 27). However, Section 4.1 documented the presence of distinct modes of bodily as well as cognitive functioning with an equivalent level of performance, which

---

[21] "The received taxonomical hierarchy is a record either of history or of the similarities that this history explains; but the simple 'classification' of individual organisms in terms of life-form precedes any possible judgment of similarity or of shared historical genesis. It is already implicit in any representation of individual organisms as alive, and thus as, for example, eating or growing, or as having arms or leaves." (Thompson 2008, 67)

[22] The closest we get is his mantra that, unlike biological concepts, a life-form is not an empirical notion: "it is a merely empirical truth, an artifact of their evolution from earlier forms, that terrestrial life-forms admit of any interesting classification into higher genera. But ... it is not a merely empirical fact, given that there are any organisms, that they fall under the particular items we were calling 'life-forms'." (Thompson 2008, 67)

therefore should not be judged differently.[23] And from my perspective, there is valuable diversity within any species. Thompson's notion of a life-form expresses the conviction of the neo-Aristotelians that one monolithic nature (with a normative-teleological impact) is shared across all members of a species, including across all of us humans – without offering a justification for this bold and problematic assumption.

Although the commitment of a neo-Aristotelian moral philosophy that adopts an essentialist and teleological understanding of a species' nature depends on which organismal characters are deemed to be part of this nature, some examples suffice to illustrate that the neo-Aristotelian approach is not only inadequate from an empirically informed point of view, but also socially harmful by adopting a stark ableism about bodily and cognitive traits. Consider this statement by Philippa Foot (2001, 16): "These free-riding individuals of a species whose members work together are just as defective as those who have defective hearing, sight, or powers of locomotion." Rosalind Hursthouse (1999, 197) quotes this statement and approvingly adds: "that is the idea I have taken over from her wholesale . . . In the context of naturalism we focus on evaluations of individual living things as or *qua* specimens of their natural kind" (Hursthouse 1999, 197). Two things stand out. First, not just an organ or physiological capacity is deemed defective, but Foot and Hursthouse call an *individual* defective whenever one aspect claimed to be teleologically necessary is absent. I deem judging an individual as either defective or non-defective inappropriate even in the case of plants and non-human animals. Yet the whole approach, attempting to ground morality, is supposed to hold for human persons as well. Indeed, Hursthouse explicitly calls some of us defective when talking about "defective human beings" (Hursthouse 1999, 214).

Second, in addition to this dehumanizing rhetoric used by some neo-Aristotelians, we already saw that there are cases where locomotion with impaired use of one's legs or impaired hearing – both of which were mentioned earlier as instances of defect by Foot and Hursthouse – yields a good level of performance. In appropriate social contexts, wheelchair users have a high degree of mobility, and deaf people signing can communicate well with each other.[24]

---

[23] Andreou (2006) challenges the account of Foot and Thompson from a similar perspective. Under the label 'mixed naturally sound types' she puts forward hypothetical examples, suggesting that a species may contain far-seeing and near-seeing individuals, as well as morally just and morally unjust individuals – where both types are naturally sound given the social species' circumstances. While noting that Foot could acknowledge that most humans exhibit mixed moral types (while still counting them as defective), Andreou's point is that the neo-Aristotelian cannot just *assume* that mixed moral types are defective.

[24] A related issue, illustrated by all their examples mentioned here, is that the neo-Aristotelians evaluate an organ or bodily activity in isolation. But we have seen from Amundson's (2000) discussion that different bodily systems can interact so as to yield some functionality or even

Consequently, one should not judge a different mode of function as inferior solely because it is a less typical mode – or a mode of function different from the one teleologically proscribed by an alleged species-wide nature. However, Foot (2001, 43) still relies on such an understanding of human nature when insisting that deaf persons are defective: "for all the diversities [*sic*] of human life, it is possible to give some quite general account of human necessities ... physical properties such as the kind of larynx that allows of the myriad sounds that make up human language, as well as the kind of hearing that can distinguish them."[25] And with the case of colour blindness, Michael Thompson also touches on neurodivergent people, but proclaiming a cognitive defect.[26]

We learned from Ron Amundson (2000) that accounts relying on the idea of 'normal function' may not only assume that only one mode of function is normal (possibly without considering the possibility and reality of alternative modes of function), but also declare the able-bodied or neurotypical mode of function as the normal one. Moreover, his examples illustrated that this one mode of function is often reinforced by social practices, while disabled and neurodivergent people can be discouraged from employing their preferred way of functioning. This way of thinking about 'normal function' may be bolstered by evolutionary considerations. Although eschewing an evolutionary or other-wise empirical perspective, the notion of a species' nature used by the natural goodness approach in neo-Aristotelian ethics is another way to declare the able-bodied or neurotypical modes as the only non-defective one.

My contention is that the neo-Aristotelian ethical 'naturalism' merely disguises personal prejudices as objective facts. Foot (2001, 38) claims that she "described the evaluation of properties and operations of plants and of animals considered in their own right, without reference to what we might desire of them ... what I call 'natural' excellence and defect." When proclaiming neurodivergent conditions such as ADHD as defective she maintains to merely report an objective fact: "there are objective, factual evaluations of such things

---

    improved performance – recall the two-legged goat and the wheelchair basketball players (Section 4.1). Likewise, the interactions between an organism and its environment or with other organisms matter, which as the social model of disability highlights includes a person's social environment. Consequently, one should not make judgements of natural goodness and defect by considering one bodily or cognitive feature in isolation.

[25] Responding to the criticism of Foot by Woodcock (2006) – see Footnote 19 above – Hacker-Wright (2009, 317) defends the neo-Aristotelian account: "Foot could comfortably embrace, I think, the claims of the Deaf community, for example, to realize distinctive human cultural goods." However, not only does Foot explicitly denounce deaf people, Hacker-Wright still upholds the idea of a species-wide nature so it is unclear how such an approach could include diverse ways of being human. Whatever traits are included in this nature – that is meant to entail normative judgements of defect – some of us will still be bodily or cognitively different.

[26] "Lameness, blindness, color-blindness, etiolation, and so forth. Such concepts may be said to express forms of natural defect." (Thompson 2008, 81)

as human sight, hearing, memory, and concentration, based on the life form of our own species" (Foot 2001, 24). But I already pointed out that she does not articulate the notion of 'function' on which she bases these judgements. And the larger neo-Aristotelian ethics tradition does not even offer a justification for the idea of a species-wide nature, and less so a reason for why certain bodily and cognitive features are postulated to be required by this human nature. Hursthouse likewise masquerades her preconceptions as objective, scientific facts:

> the truth of such evaluations of living things does not depend in any way on my wants, interests, or values, nor indeed on 'ours'. They are, in the most straightforward sense of the term, 'objective'; indeed, given that botany, zoology, ethology, etc. are sciences, they are scientific. Readers unfamiliar with such evaluations, or inclined to think that they necessarily have something to do with approval or praise, should take note of the many excellent gardening and nature programmes available on television. (Hursthouse 1999, 202–203)

Hursthouse does not point to any biologist making goodness as opposed to defect judgements; indeed, the biological disciplines she mentions are not in the business of passing normative evaluations judging a whole individual to be defective. Instead, all she appeals to are gardening and nature shows, even though the anthropocentric perspective that may be taken therein is not scientific and certainly not value-free.

As opposed to a proper understanding of human variation, where traits contribute more or less to biological functioning or an individual's flourishing, we have encountered the notion of natural or Aristotelian 'necessities,' which have to be fully present, while any variation from them prompts the judgement of a defective person. And we have been confronted with examples of cognitive and other neurodivergent conditions, including colour blindness, reduced hearing capacities, and reduced memory and concentration, which are alleged to render some of us defective. Given that the natural goodness approach is ultimately after judging moral reasoning and character, based on capacities for rational reasoning, the account is committed to counting quite a few people with developmental and cognitive disabilities as defective humans – based on no empirical considerations about such persons' actual capacities and integration in social life. Moreover, Philippa Foot labels non-rational individuals "sub-rational" beings (Foot 2001, 27 & 41). Applied to humans, such cognitive inferiority language dehumanizes some of us. And it echoes the many instances in the history of philosophy where women and especially Black and Indigenous people were deemed to be not fully human and even subhuman based on the claim of them lacking rational capacities.

4.3 Whither Human Nature?

Among the criticisms of the natural goodness approach in neo-Aristotelian virtue ethics mentioned in the previous subsection, my core target was its essentialist and teleological concept of human nature. More generally, I objected to the idea of a monolithic, species-wide nature for any species – which also was used to render false and even socially harmful evaluative judgments of natural defects, including regarding a person's cognitive features. Even without a normative agenda of ascribing defects, a monolithic construal of a species' nature is at odds with its diversity, in particular our human cognitive diversity. This brings us to the very idea of human nature. Given that the label 'human nature' tends to suggest a universal nature, often understood to consist of biological or other essential features (e.g., Pinker 2002; Tooby and Cosmides 2015),[27] one may wonder whether one should use the notion of human nature at all – possibly discarding it as a defective concept – or whether a revisionary concept of human nature can do justice to human diversity (Brigandt 2024b; Hull 1986).

One perspective that attempts to capture biological variation is the account of species by Christopher Austin (2019), which although not specifically meant as an account of 'human nature' applies to our species as well and then has implications for the nature of the human species. Noteworthy, Austin endorses an essentialist and neo-Aristotelian account, where this is not an instance of neo-Aristotelian ethics but of neo-Aristotelian metaphysics. Against longstanding criticism that species are not natural kinds or in any case not natural kinds with intrinsic essences (Brigandt 2024a), Austin's agenda is to recover a construal of species as natural kinds with purely intrinsic essences – while still attempting to do justice to within-species variation and such phenomena as phenotypic plasticity (explained in Section 3.2).[28] In line with the recent philosophical enthusiasm about dispositions, including in the philosophy of biology (Brigandt et al. 2023; Hüttemann and Kaiser 2018; Suárez 2023b), Austin's central tenet is that all members of a species share the same disposition to develop in a certain fashion. He suggests that this disposition has its basis in an organism's developmental modules (and is thereby an intrinsic essence).

---

[27] Meynell (2020) objects to the idea of a universal human nature as endorsed by some evolutionary psychologists on the grounds of it being ableist by leaving out some neurodivergent people (e.g., deeming persons without certain mental modules claimed to be essential as not having fully human natures).

[28] Prominent objections to species as natural kinds argued instead that each species is an individual (Ghiselin 1974; Hull 1978). Accounts that endeavoured to still construe species as natural kinds have employed non-intrinsic properties (as characterizing the identity of a species), including the relational properties of having the same ancestry as, being able to interbreed with, and occupying the same ecological niche as another organism (Brigandt 2009, 2024a).

Crucially, Austin eschews the outdated idea that the species essence entails that one species-typical phenotype develops. Instead, due to phenotypic plasticity, an organism's developmental modules are able to generate a variety of phenotypic outcomes, depending on the environmental and other circumstances outside the organism. A species thereby exhibits one disposition with the developmental capacity for all phenotypic outcomes that are possible for this species. As an Aristotelian disposition, it is teleologically directed toward any such developmental outcome. As a true neo-Aristotelian metaphysician, Austin throws in some good old-fashioned hylomorphism. The form consisting of a species-wide, goal-directed disposition is multiply realized in matter, so that different organisms of a species can have different developmental modules.

My topic is whether Austin's (2019) metaphysical account of the nature of the human species adequately incorporates considerations about human diversity.[29] First, I note shortcomings regarding *appreciating* human diversity. Although Austin acknowledges that the form/essence of the human species can generate a wide range of human variation, one could wonder whether this form actually exists – as something over and above the various bodily features – or whether it is merely postulated as something creating an abstract unity across diverse human organisms. More importantly for my purposes, Austin's essentialist approach privileges this form over the diversity exhibited by us humans. While this is not a version of typological thinking that would postulate one natural state for a species, it still has elements of what I criticized as a 'typological approach' in Section 2.1, insofar as Austin's account makes concrete humans and their bodily, cognitive, and behavioural features – which is what exhibits the diversity to be appreciated – subordinated to the abstract form or type that is the focus of Austin's agenda. Moreover, his essentialist account obscures that the current range of human diversity (provided by one dispositional form) is contingent and *subject to change*.

Another way in which Austin's account falls short of a proper appreciation of human diversity stems from his adoption of a teleological perspective. To be sure, his version of teleology does not privilege some developmental trajectories or correspondingly some developmental outcomes over others – unlike the natural goodness approach from the previous subsection. Still, viewing developmental trajectories through a teleological lens privileges the developmental outcome over the changing traits leading up to some (not actually unchanging) 'outcome.' These changing biological traits are as real as the outcome, and also have to be the focus as they are part of human biological diversity. Indeed, one

---

[29] Sterelny (2018) also has critical considerations about a human nature with an intrinsic essence, with Devitt (2008) as his critical target.

important aspect of human diversity is the various *contingent* events that underlie this diversity. However, Austin's intrinsic essentialism views developmental trajectories as teleologically governed by features internal to an organism, as opposed to the varied and contingent interactions between an organism and its environment as well as other organisms.[30] Such contingent and complex interactions are particularly important for understanding the nature of human *cognitive* diversity.

Second, Austin's account clearly fails at *explaining* human diversity (regardless of whether such an explanation is important to him). This stems from his exclusive focus on intrinsic essences. To address past criticisms of construing species as having intrinsic essences, Austin (2019, ch.2) separates the question of what makes an organism a member of its species (which he sets out to answer in terms of *intrinsic* properties) from the question of what makes a biological taxon a species as opposed to some other category (where the relational and other *extrinsic* properties that other accounts have emphasized would be relevant). Since metaphysical accounts of species as natural kinds felt it important to include extrinsic properties, one may doubt whether Austin's separation strategy yields an adequate account of the ontology of species (Brigandt 2024a). In any case, exclusively focusing on intrinsic properties robs Austin of the resources to *explain* human diversity. For it is biological and social interactions external to an individual person that generate human diversity and explain how diversity is continuously being transformed – including human cognitive diversity, as detailed in Section 3.2.

Beyond essentialist accounts of the nature of the human species in neo-Aristotelian metaphysics or ethics, especially the philosophy of biology has moved toward accounts of human nature that are non-essentialist and capture human diversity (Kronfeldner et al. 2014; Mameli 2024; Stotz and Griffiths 2018). A noteworthy approach has been put forward by Grant Ramsey, which he has elaborated and defended in his Cambridge Element *Human Nature* (2023). He contrasts his approach with what he calls trait bin accounts of human nature. The latter sort various traits into those that are part of human nature (regardless of whether these are conceptualized as essential traits) and those that do not make up human nature. Such a trait bin account faces difficulties in capturing the full extent of human diversity, which is one reason for Ramsey to instead favour his trait cluster account of human nature. While addressing relationships among traits, the account goes beyond correlations of present traits by capturing all possible life histories: "Human nature is the pattern of trait clusters within

---

[30] In contrast to Austin construing developmental potential as an intrinsic disposition, there have been accounts of dispositions in biology emphasizing that many dispositions are extrinsic dispositions (Brigandt et al. 2023; Hüttemann and Kaiser 2018; Suárez 2023a).

the totality of extant human possible life histories" (Ramsey 2023, 21). This covers complex, conditional probabilities that map out how likely it is for a particular trait to arise at some future life-history stage depending on what the previous circumstances are, including a person's bodily features and environmental conditions. Although restricting this account of human nature to the life histories that are possible for *extant* humans, the spirit is to acknowledge that past humans had and future humans will have somewhat different life-history potentials, so that the nature of our species has been changing, while Ramsey's account is about our nature here and now.

Stephen Downes (2016) raises the legitimate doubt that while covering all sorts of human traits, an account of human nature like Ramsey's is not particularly interesting as it fails to perform an explanatory function (see also Sterelny 2018). By Downes's lights, the explanatory potential does not stem from Ramsey's very account of human nature, but from the evolutionary and other scientific resources he draws from, such as life-history theory. More important for my desideratum of doing justice to human diversity is this potential worry: I have been critical of Austin's (2019) metaphysical account of the human species, which attempts to capture variation in terms of a disposition for all possible phenotypic outcomes across the species. But isn't Ramsey's (2023) account in terms of all possible life histories just the same, albeit without embracing the label of an 'essence'? My verdict is that there are some fundamental differences, that make Ramsey's account suitable to capture human diversity, including cognitive diversity. First, whereas Austin upholds a teleological construal of developmental trajectories that are geared toward some outcome, so as to privilege phenotypic outcomes, Ramsey's trait relations treat traits at any life-history stage equally, also making room for contingency throughout development. Second, Austin postulates one disposition (Aristotelian form) shared by all members of the human species. In contrast, Ramsey's starting point is the life histories that are possible for an individual person – where there can be significant differences across persons – and human nature is no more than the collection of all these individual potentialities. Third, a central tenet of Austin is that the essence of the human species is intrinsic, consisting exclusively of internal, bodily traits. Yet Ramsey permits all kinds of traits to form trait clusters, including relational properties. Indeed, he rebukes the objection that his account was too permissive in including various traits or that an account of human nature would have to focus on our core while excluding the veneer. From my perspective, the between-person interactions and other relational properties that Ramsey's account includes are crucial for understanding how human cognitive variation is generated and maintained.

Another valuable approach to human nature has been advanced by Maria Kronfeldner in *What's Left of Human Nature? A Post-Essentialist, Pluralist, and Interactive Account of a Contested Concept* (2018). Kronfeldner's starting point is that traditional accounts of human nature were meant to fulfill three tasks: accounting for what makes humans members of their particular species, describing the characteristic properties of humans, and explaining the presence and historical origination of these properties. She convincingly argues that any single concept of human nature cannot accomplish all three tasks and by targeting all three is bound to result in an essentialist or otherwise problematic account of human nature, at least by offering a flawed account of some humans. Consequently, Kronfeldner puts forward three accounts of human nature, each geared toward a different task: (1) a classificatory nature, (2) a descriptive nature, and (3) an explanatory nature. Although it is less obvious to me that her account of the descriptive nature – covering the properties routinely studied by biology, cognitive science, and social science – is inclusive enough to cover the full range of human diversity (unlike Ramsey's account), her explanatory nature rightly includes features that are biologically as well as socially transmitted. The core reason why I point to Kronfeldner's (2018) approach is this: even though she is not only happy to uphold the very idea of human nature but in fact endorse three concepts of human nature, she forcefully rejects any *normative* concept of human nature, because by proclaiming some traits as normal or ideal it would dehumanize some of us as being abnormal or inferior.

I personally have no ambition to develop or endorse an account of human nature. For as mentioned at the beginning of this subsection, many traditional accounts of human nature have tended to focus on (allegedly) universal features of humans, including aspects of some cognitive architecture. And the use of the word (human) 'nature' tends to even prompt the idea of an essence or one normal way of being. At a minimum, any potential concept of human nature must conform to two points. First, it should fully capture the varieties of being human, including cognitive and behavioural diversity. Second, it should not uphold normative tenets about what would qualify as normal (e.g., normal cognitive functioning), as these are our value-judgements that do not follow from an objective nature and – as illustrated in Sections 4.1 and 4.2 – accounts that tacitly or explicitly assumed a nature with a universal standard for bodily or cognitive functioning are biologically uninformed about the diversity of functioning and normatively ableist or otherwise fail to do justice to humans and their diversity.

5 Conclusion

While this Cambridge Element has addressed topics ranging from empirical science to neo-Aristotelian ethics in philosophy, the underlying theme has been the question: How to understand human cognitive diversity? More precisely, the critical issue is how to *properly* scientifically represent, explain, and philosophically appreciate and value cognitive diversity.

Across the cognitive and behavioural sciences, there are a vast number of investigative methodologies and explanatory agendas. To get a sense of the limitations of some approaches – including their larger societal impacts – I contrasted research on sex differences in the brain with several alternative research methodologies that are better able to capture and explain cognitive diversity. Agendas that are primarily interested in cognitive *difference* between some groups (be it sex, gender, or racial differences in cognition) tend to adopt what I called a 'typological approach,' which scientifically represents an average trait for each group. This fails to represent the trait variation within the group – as an important aspect of human *diversity*. And there is the danger that this average is conveyed to be some type that would be representative of everyone within the group, as it happens when cognitive science researchers talk about 'the female brain type' (as opposed to the 'male brain type') or claim that there is 'the female brain' (as opposed to 'the male brain'). We also encountered several other methodological agendas that are more in line with my call for understanding human cognitive diversity. One clear alternative to attempting to corroborate a package deal of female-typical traits that are reliably correlated across women is to investigate and represent complex distributions between many individual neurocognitive traits (across all persons), for example, in terms of most of us having some 'mosaic brain' (that differs from many other mosaic brains). Another alternative is to charter the variation within a group, while also using further analytical categories than sex and gender. The fields of cultural psychology and cultural psychology illustrated such an approach. Although there have been accounts in cultural psychology that have portrayed a typological vision by contrasting 'Westerners' and 'Asians,' I documented fruitful ongoing research in this domain that uses a variety of analytical categories to analyze the dimensions of human cognitive diversity, including SES, gender, religion, and culture.

My discussion emphasized how the use of different representational and analytical frameworks in cognitive science can matter to society. Typological representations, which portray one group as a monolithic whole and emphasize differences between groups, are prone to reinforce societal stereotypes about such groups. Beyond past research on alleged cognitive differences between races, this also holds for ongoing research that focuses on gender differences in cognition. We saw that many cognitive traits attributed to some groups have a social valence. For instance, in many societies, the mathematical and spatial reasoning abilities that brain organization theory ascribes to men are associated with privileged occupations and social positions, compared to the empathetic and nurturing abilities ascribed to women. This is the reason why reinforcing stereotypes (which in reality do not hold for everyone within some group) can have harmful societal impacts. As a result, research approaches that investigate and depict more of the actually existing human cognitive variation and diversity not only offer more empirical detail, but can also function as a social-political tool for undermining harmful racial, gender, and other social stereotypes.

Focusing on a single dimension of difference (e.g., gender) not only leaves out other dimensions of variation but also suggests that this one factor is privileged. This brings us to the explanation of human cognitive diversity. There are approaches such as the study of sex differences in the brain that are primarily interested in the biological contribution to cognitive differences. This obviously falls short of investigating the causal role of social-environmental factors on cognition. And since such social-environmental features (including a person's past behaviour and experiences) can impact a person's neurophysiology, neuroanatomy, and other bodily features, there is no 'biological contribution' to cognitive variation independently of social-environmental contributions that could be uncovered by some research approach. Instead, I documented different examples of work in the cognitive and behavioural sciences that not only conceptually eschew a nature-nurture dichotomy, but actively investigate the interplay between various features. This includes research investigating neuroplasticity (as a special case of phenotypic plasticity), including research in cultural neuroscience that sheds light on how different cultural and religious contexts influence neurophysiology. I also pointed to research using the construct of sex/gender or gender/sex for contexts where it is not feasible or fruitful to separate sex (as a more biological feature) and gender (as a more social feature), basically because of the mutual influences of sex and gender. In the case of Joseph Henrich's explanatory hypothesis of how the globally peculiar WEIRD psychology (of people from Western, educated, rich, and democratic countries) historically originated in the first place, we encountered an explanatory framework that not only addresses regional cognitive variation, but also the historical change in cognitive patterns. Henrich's explanatory framework envisions the interplay between social-institutional and psychological features, which engage in ongoing feedback loops. I also pointed to similar work on human cognitive niche construction, as well as accounts emphasizing the role of cognitive plasticity for variation in human moral cognition.

Although for purposes of simplicity, I discussed the scientific representation and the explanation of human cognitive diversity in different sections, one should note that these issues are not unrelated. While there are many studies that focus on measuring and describing cognitive variation, even in these contexts it can matter what potential explanatory framework a researcher has in mind. For the explanatory framework envisioned impacts what kinds of data are collected and what analytical categories are used to analyze and represent the finding. Moreover, it matters to society at large which explanatory frameworks are being pursued. Research that is only interested in uncovering the role that biological sex has on cognitive differences feeds into longstanding perceptions that cognitive differences are largely biological. This motivates the idea that social reforms targeting social inequities are moot, or even that social hierarchies are to be seen as natural – assumptions that historically have influenced public policies. In contrast, research that explains cognitive diversity in terms of a variety of factors, including social-environmental factors and the interactions among individuals, reveals to the public that cognitive variation is contingent and mutable. This is especially the case for explanations of how cognitive diversity has historically originated and how the shape of cognitive variation is changing. Most importantly, such explanatory frameworks offer potential ways for how public policies can improve mental health and reduce mental health disparities. Explanations that reveal how social conditions and a person's behaviour and experiences create risk factors for psychiatric symptoms can be used to develop preventive public health policies. To be sure, there are many practical obstacles to arriving at replicable findings that capture the full range of human cognitive diversity and its various underlying causes, most prominently financial hurdles. Still, my considerations advances in Sections 2.3 and 3.3 call for society to foster scientific methodologies and studies that are better at measuring and explaining cognitive diversity.

In the context of appreciating and positively valuing human cognitive diversity, my discussion also addressed cognitive disability and the notion of neurodiversity. Rather than viewing all neurodivergent conditions as abnormal, neurodiversity encourages us to consider many of them part of normal human cognitive diversity. We saw that diversity of bodily and cognitive function is a biological reality, with many different modes of functioning being able to yield the same level of functioning. In contrast, the idea of 'normal function' has tended to falsely construe the able-bodied mode of functioning as the normal one, while attempting to socially impose it on disabled and neurodivergent persons. This misguided vision can also be found in contemporary moral philosophy. I rejected the natural goodness approach in neo-Aristotelian virtue ethics that endorses a species-universal standard for its failure to appreciate diversity. It even upholds an ableist account by considering any bodily and cognitive feature that does not conform to the neo-Aristotelian species-universal standard a natural defect. Such an essentialist construal of the human life-form or nature raises questions about using the notion of human nature at all, given that human nature has traditionally been viewed as something shared by all humans. While I do not see much value in an account of human nature, I argued that at minimum any concept of human nature must do justice to human diversity – including cognitive diversity – and must not have normative connotations that would devalue or even dehumanize some of us.

We humans are diverse. Our cognitive diversity has been changing in evolution and recent history. But also our thinking about cognitive differences and our cognitive variation has been historically changing, including in the behavioural and cognitive sciences. Here is hope that our ordinary and scientific understanding will grow more and more toward properly understanding and appreciating human cognitive diversity.

References

Ainsworth, C. (2015). Sex redefined: The idea of two sexes is simplistic. Biologists now think there is a wider spectrum than that. *Nature*, 518-(7539): 288–91.

Amundson, R. (2000). Against normal function. *Studies in History and Philosophy of Biological and Biomedical Sciences*, 31(1): 33–53.

Amundson, R. and Lauder, G. V. (1994). Function without purpose: The uses of causal role functions in evolutionary biology. *Biology and Philosophy*, 9(4): 443–69.

Anderson, E. (1995). Knowledge, human interests, and objectivity in feminist epistemology. *Philosophical Topics*, 23(2): 27–58.

Anderson, M. L. (2014). *After Phrenology: Neural Reuse and the Interactive Brain*, Cambridge, MA: MIT Press.

Andreou, C. (2006). Getting on in a varied world. *Social Theory and Practice*, 32(1): 61–73.

Arnold, A. P. (2009). The organizational-activational hypothesis as the foundation for a unified theory of sexual differentiation of all mammalian tissues. *Hormones and Behavior*, 55(5): 570–78.

Austin, C. J. (2019). *Essence in the Age of Evolution: A New Theory of Natural Kinds*, New York: Routledge.

Bao, Y. and Pöppel, E. (2012). Anthropological universals and cultural specifics: Conceptual and methodological challenges in cultural neuroscience. *Neuroscience & Biobehavioral Reviews*, 36(9): 2143–46.

Barnes, E. (2016). *The Minority Body: A Theory of Disability*, Oxford: Oxford University Press.

Baron-Cohen, S. (2002). The extreme male brain theory of autism. *Trends in Cognitive Sciences*, 6(6): 248–54.

  (2003). *The Essential Difference: Male And Female Brains and the Truth about Autism*, New York: Basic Books.

Becker, J. B., Berkley, K. J., Geary, N. et al., eds. (2007). *Sex Differences in the Brain: From Genes to Behavior*, New York: Oxford University Press.

Bleier, R. (1984). *Science and Gender: A Critique of Biology and Its Theories on Women, 2nd ed.*, New York: Pergamon Press.

Bluhm, R. (2012). Beyond neurosexism: Is it possible to defend the female brain? In R. Bluhm, A. J. Jacobson, and H. L. Maibom, eds., *Neurofeminism: Issues at the Intersection of Feminist Theory and Cognitive Science*. New York: Palgrave Macmillan, pp. 230–45.

(2020). Neurosexism and our understanding of sex differences in the brain. In S. Crasnow and K. Intemann, eds., *The Routledge Handbook of Feminist Philosophy of Science*. New York: Routledge, pp. 316–27.

Boorse, C. (1997). A rebuttal on health. In J. M. Humber and R. F. Almeder, eds., *What Is Disease?* Totowa, NJ: Humana Press, pp. 1–134.

Brigandt, I. (2005). The instinct concept of the early Konrad Lorenz. *Journal of the History of Biology*, 38(3): 571–608.

(2009). Natural kinds in evolution and systematics: Metaphysical and epistemological considerations. *Acta Biotheoretica*, 57(1–2): 77–97.

(2015a). Evolutionary developmental biology and the limits of philosophical accounts of mechanistic explanation. In P.-A. Braillard and C. Malaterre, eds., *Explanation in Biology: An Enquiry into the Diversity of Explanatory Patterns in the Life Sciences*. Dordrecht: Springer, pp. 135–73.

(2015b). Social values influence the adequacy conditions of scientific theories: Beyond inductive risk. *Canadian Journal of Philosophy*, 45(3): 326–56.

(2022a). Engaging with science, values, and society: Introduction. *Canadian Journal of Philosophy*, 52(3): 223–26.

(2022b). How to philosophically tackle kinds without talking about "natural kinds". *Canadian Journal of Philosophy*, 52(3): 356–79.

(2024a). Biological species. In K. Koslicki and M. Raven, eds., *The Routledge Handbook of Essence in Philosophy*. New York: Routledge, pp. 276–90.

(2024b). Evolutionstheorie und Naturalismus. In M. Zichy, ed., *Handbuch Menschenbilder*. Wiesbaden: Springer, pp. 601–20.

Brigandt, I. and Rosario, E. (2020). Strategic conceptual engineering for epistemic and social aims. In A. Burgess, H. Cappelen, and D. Plunkett, eds., *Conceptual Engineering and Conceptual Ethics*. Oxford: Oxford University Press, pp. 100–24.

Brigandt, I., Villegas, C., Love, A. C., and Nuño de la Rosa, L. (2023). Evolvability as a disposition: Philosophical distinctions and scientific implications. In T. F. Hansen, D. Houle, M. Pavličev, and C. Pélabon, eds., *Evolvability: A Unifying Concept in Evolutionary Biology?* Cambridge, MA: MIT Press, pp. 55–72.

Brizendine, L. (2006). *The Female Brain*, New York: Three Rivers Press.

(2010). *The Male Brain*, New York: Broadway Books.

Brown, M. J. (2020). *Science and Moral Imagination: A New Ideal for Values in Science*, Pittsburgh: University of Pittsburgh Press.

Brown, G. R., Dickins, T. E., Sear, R., and Laland, K. N. (2011). Evolutionary accounts of human behavioural diversity. *Philosophical Transactions of the Royal Society B: Biological Sciences*, 366(1563): 313–24.

Buchanan, A. and Powell, R. (2018). *The Evolution of Moral Progress: A Biocultural Theory*, Oxford: Oxford University Press.

Buller, D. J. (2005). *Adapting Minds: Evolutionary Psychology and the Persistent Quest for Human Nature*, Cambridge, MA: MIT Press.

  (2006). Evolutionary psychology: A critique. In E. Sober, ed., *Conceptual Issues in Evolutionary Biology*, 3rd ed. Cambridge, MA: MIT Press, pp. 197–214.

Burgess, A., Cappelen, H., and Plunkett, D., eds. (2020). *Conceptual Engineering and Conceptual Ethics*, Oxford: Oxford University Press.

Chapman, R. (2023). *Empire of Normality: Neurodiversity and Capitalism*, London: Pluto Press.

Chekroud, A. M., Ward, E. J., Rosenberg, M. D., and Holmes, A. J. (2016). Patterns in the human brain mosaic discriminate males from females. *Proceedings of the National Academy of Sciences*, 113(14): E1968.

Cheon, B. K., Im, D.-M., Harada, T. et al. (2011). Cultural influences on neural basis of intergroup empathy. *NeuroImage*, 57(2): 642–50.

Chiang, J. J., Saphire-Bernstein, S., Kim, H. S., Sherman, D. K., and Taylor, S. E. (2012). Cultural differences in the link between supportive relationships and proinflammatory cytokines. *Social Psychological and Personality Science*, 4(5): 511–20.

Chiao, J. Y., ed. (2009). *Cultural Neuroscience: Cultural Influences on Brain Function*, Amsterdam: Elsevier.

Chiao, J. Y., Cheon, B. K., Pornpattananangkul, N., Mrazek, A. J., and Blizinsky, K. D. (2013). Cultural neuroscience: Understanding human diversity. In M. J. Gelfand, C.-y. Chiu, and Y.-y. Hong, eds., *Advances in Culture and Psychology*. Oxford: Oxford University Press, pp. 1–77.

Choudhury, S. and Kirmayer, L. J. (2009). Cultural neuroscience and psychopathology: Prospects for cultural psychiatry. In J. Y. Chiao, ed., *Progress in Brain Research*: Amsterdam: Elsevier, pp. 263–83.

Choudhury, S. and Slaby, J. (2012). *Critical Neuroscience: A Handbook of the Social and Cultural Contexts of Neuroscience*, Chichester: Wiley-Blackwell.

Chung, W. C. J. and Auger, A. P. (2013). Gender differences in neurodevelopment and epigenetics. *Pflügers Archiv – European Journal of Physiology*, 465(5): 573–84.

Clune-Taylor, C. (2020). Is sex socially constructed? In S. Crasnow and K. Intemann, eds., *The Routledge Handbook of Feminist Philosophy of Science*. New York: Routledge, pp. 187–200.

Cohen, A. B. (2009). Many forms of culture. *American Psychologist*, 64(3): 194–204.

Cohen, A. B. and Hill, P. C. (2007). Religion as culture: Religious individualism and collectivism among American Catholics, Jews, and Protestants. *Journal of Personality*, 75(4): 709–42.

Cohen, D. and Kitayama, S., eds. (2019). *Handbook of Cultural Psychology*, *2nd ed.*, New York: Guilford Press.

Cohen, D., Nisbett, R. E., Bowdle, B. F., and Schwarz, N. (1996). Insult, aggression, and the southern culture of honor: An "experimental ethnography." *Journal of Personality and Social Psychology*, 70(5): 945–60.

Curley, J. P., Jensen, C. L., Mashoodh, R., and Champagne, F. A. (2011). Social influences on neurobiology and behavior: Epigenetic effects during development. *Psychoneuroendocrinology*, 36(3): 352–71.

Daniels, N. (1987). Justice and health care. In D. VanDeVeer and T. Regan, eds., *Health Care Ethics: An Introduction*. Philadelphia: Temple University Press, pp. 290–325.

Dar-Nimrod, I. and Heine, S. J. (2011). Genetic essentialism: On the deceptive determinism of DNA. *Psychological Bulletin*, 137(5): 800–18.

de Greck, M., Shi, Z., Wang, G. et al. (2012). Culture modulates brain activity during empathy with anger. *NeuroImage*, 59(3): 2871–82.

de Melo-Martín, I. and Intemann, K. (2018). *The Fight against Doubt: How to Bridge the Gap Between Scientists and the Public*, Oxford: Oxford University Press.

Devitt, M. (2008). Resurrecting biological essentialism. *Philosophy of Science*, 75(3): 344–82.

Doan, M. D. and Fenton, A. (2013). Embodying autistic cognition: Towards reconceiving certain "autism-related" behavioral atypicalities as functional. In J. L. Anderson and S. Cushing, eds., *The Philosophy of Autism*. Lanham: Rowman & Littlefield, pp. 47–71.

Dokumacı, A. (2023). *Activist Affordances How Disabled People Improvise More Habitable Worlds*, Durham: Duke University Press.

Douglas, H. E. (2009). *Science, Policy, and the Value-Free Ideal*, Pittsburgh: University of Pittsburgh Press.

Downes, S. M. (2016). Confronting variation in the social and behavioral sciences. *Philosophy of Science*, 83(5): 909–20.

Dussauge, I. and Kaiser, A. (2012). Re-queering the brain. In R. Bluhm, A. J. Jacobson, and H. L. Maibom, eds., *Neurofeminism: Issues at the Intersection of Feminist Theory and Cognitive Science*. New York: Palgrave Macmillan, pp. 121–44.

Eichler, M. (1988). *Nonsexist Research Methods: A Practical Guide*, Boston, MA: Allen & Unwin.

Eliot, L. (2009). *Pink Brain, Blue Brain: How Small Differences Grow into Troublesome Gaps – and What We Can Do about It*, New York: Houghton Mifflin Harcourt.

(2011). The trouble with sex differences. *Neuron*, 72(6): 895–98.

Elliott, K. C. (2017). *A Tapestry of Values: An Introduction to Values in Science*, Oxford: Oxford University Press.

(2022). *Values in Science*, Cambridge: Cambridge University Press.

Elliott, K. C. and McKaughan, D. J. (2014). Nonepistemic values and the multiple goals of science. *Philosophy of Science*, 81(1): 1–21.

Ellis, B. J. and Boyce, W. T. (2008). Biological sensitivity to context. *Current Directions in Psychological Science*, 17(3): 183–87.

Ellis, B. J., Boyce, W. T., Belsky, J., Bakermans-Kranenburg, M. J., and van Ijzendoorn, M. H. (2011). Differential susceptibility to the environment: An evolutionary-neurodevelopmental theory. *Development and Psychopathology*, 23(1): 7–28.

Else-Quest, N. M. and Hyde, J. S. (2020). Implementing intersectionality in psychology with quantitative methods. In S. Crasnow and K. Intemann, eds., *The Routledge Handbook of Feminist Philosophy of Science*. New York: Routledge, pp. 340–52.

Fausto-Sterling, A. (1992). *Myths of Gender: Biological Theories about Women and Men, revised edition*, New York: Basic Books.

(2012). *Sex/Gender: Biology in a Social World*, New York: Routledge.

Fehr, C. and Plaisance, K. S. (2010). Socially relevant philosophy of science: An introduction. *Synthese*, 177(3): 301–16.

Fenton, A. and Krahn, T. (2007). Autism, neurodiversity and equality beyond the "normal." *Journal of Ethics in Mental Health*, 2(2): 1–6.

Fernández, A. L. and Evans, J., eds. (2022). *Understanding Cross-Cultural Neuropsychology: Science, Testing, and Challenges*, London: Routledge.

Fincher, C. L., Thornhill, R., Murray, D. R., and Schaller, M. (2008). Pathogen prevalence predicts human cross-cultural variability in individualism/collectivism. *Proceedings of the Royal Society B: Biological Sciences*, 275-(1640): 1279–85.

Fine, C. (2010). *Delusions of Gender: How Our Minds, Society, and Neurosexism Create Difference*, New York: W. W. Norton.

(2017). *Testosterone Rex: Myths of Sex, Science, and Society*, New York: W. W. Norton.

Fine, C., Dupré, J., and Joel, D. (2017). Sex-linked behavior: Evolution, stability, and variability. *Trends in Cognitive Sciences*, 21(9): 666–73.

Flynn, J. R. (2007). *What Is Intelligence? Beyond the Flynn Effect*, Cambridge: Cambridge University Press.

Fodor, J. A. (1983). *The Modularity of Mind*, Cambridge, MA: MIT Press.

Foot, P. (2001). *Natural Goodness*, Oxford: Oxford University Press.

Gannett, L. (2004). The biological reification of race. *British Journal for the Philosophy of Science*, 55(2): 323–45.

Gatzke-Kopp, L. M. (2016). Diversity and representation: Key issues for psychophysiological science. *Psychophysiology*, 53(1): 3–13.

Gelfand, M. J., Chiu, C.-y., and Hong, Y.-y., eds. (2013). *Advances in Culture and Psychology*, Oxford: Oxford University Press.

Ghiselin, M. T. (1974). A radical solution to the species problem. *Systematic Zoology*, 23: 536–44.

Gilbert, S. F., Bosch, T. C. G., and Ledon-Rettig, C. (2015). Eco-Evo-Devo: Developmental symbiosis and developmental plasticity as evolutionary agents. *Nature Reviews Genetics*, 16(10): 611–22.

Gould, S. J. (1996). *The Mismeasure of Man*, 2nd ed., New York: W. W. Norton.

Griffiths, P. E. (2001). Genetic information: A metaphor in search of a theory. *Philosophy of Science*, 68: 394–412.

(2002). What is innateness? *The Monist*, 85: 70–85.

Gurian, M. and Stevens, K. (2005). *The Minds of Boys: Saving Our Sons from Falling behind in School and Life*, San Francisco, CA: Jossey-Bass.

Hacker-Wright, J. (2009). What is natural about Foot's ethical naturalism? *Ratio*, 22(3): 308–21.

Hacking, I. (1999). *The Social Construction of What?* Cambridge, MA: Harvard University Press.

Halpern, D. F. (2012). *Sex Differences in Cognitive Abilities*, 4th ed., New York: Psychology Press.

Hamilton, C. (2008). *Cognition and Sex Differences*, Basingstoke: Palgrave Macmillan.

Heine, S. J. (2016). *DNA Is Not Destiny: The Remarkable, Completely Misunderstood Relationship Between You and Your Genes*, New York: W. W. Norton.

Heine, S. J., Dar-Nimrod, I., Cheung, B. Y., and Proulx, T. (2017). Essentially biased: Why people are fatalistic about genes. In J. M. Olson, ed., *Advances in Experimental Social Psychology*. Cambridge, MA: Academic Press, pp. 137–92.

Henrich, J. (2020). *The WEIRDest People in the World: How the West Became Psychologically Peculiar and Particularly Prosperous*, New York: Picador.

Henrich, J., Heine, S. J., and Norenzayan, A. (2010). The weirdest people in the world? *Behavioral and Brain Sciences*, 33(2–3): 61–83.

Herrnstein, R. J. and Murray, C. (1994). *The Bell Curve: Intelligence and Class Structure in American Life*, New York: Free Press.

Hines, M. (2004). *Brain Gender*, Oxford: Oxford University Press.

Hoffman, G. (2012). What, if anything, can neuroscience tell us about gender differences? In R. Bluhm, A. J. Jacobson, and H. L. Maibom, eds., *Neurofeminism: Issues at the Intersection of Feminist Theory and Cognitive Science*. New York: Palgrave Macmillan, pp. 30–55.

Hull, D. L. (1978). A matter of individuality. *Philosophy of Science*, 45: 335–60.

   (1986). On human nature. *PSA: Proceedings of the Biennial Meeting of the Philosophy of Science Association*, 1986(2): 3–13.

Hursthouse, R. (1999). *On Virtue Ethics*, Oxford: Oxford University Press.

Hüttemann, A. and Kaiser, M. I. (2018). Potentiality in biology. In K. Engelhard and M. Quante, eds., *Handbook of Potentiality*. Dordrecht: Springer, pp. 401–28.

Hyde, J. S. (2005). The gender similarities hypothesis. *American Psychologist*, 60(6): 581–92.

Hyde, J. S., Bigler, R. S., Joel, D., Tate, C. C., and van Anders, S. M. (2019). The future of sex and gender in psychology: Five challenges to the gender binary. *American Psychologist*, 74(2): 171–93.

Intemann, K. (2015). Distinguishing between legitimate and illegitimate values in climate modeling. *European Journal for Philosophy of Science*, 5(2): 217–32.

Jaarsma, P. and Welin, S. (2012). Autism as a natural human variation: Reflections on the claims of the neurodiversity movement. *Health Care Analysis*, 20(1): 20–30.

Joel, D. (2011). Male or female? Brains are intersex. *Frontiers in Integrative Neuroscience*, 5: 57.

   (2021). Beyond the binary: Rethinking sex and the brain. *Neuroscience & Biobehavioral Reviews*, 122: 165–75.

Joel, D., Berman, Z., Tavor, I. et al. (2015). Sex beyond the genitalia: The human brain mosaic. *Proceedings of the National Academy of Sciences*, 112(50): 15468–73.

Joel, D. and Fausto-Sterling, A. (2016). Beyond sex differences: New approaches for thinking about variation in brain structure and function. *Philosophical Transactions of the Royal Society B: Biological Sciences*, 371(1688): 20150451.

Joel, D., Persico, A., Salhov, M. et al. (2018). Analysis of human brain structure reveals that the brain "types" typical of males are also typical of females, and vice versa. *Frontiers in Human Neuroscience*, 12: 399.

Joel, D. and Vikhanski, L. (2019). *Gender Mosaic: Beyond the Myth of the Male and Female Brain*, London: Endeavour.

Jordan-Young, R. M. (2010). *Brain Storm: The Flaws in the Science of Sex Differences*, Cambridge, MA: Harvard University Press.

Jordan-Young, R. M. and Rumiati, R. I. (2012). Hardwired for sexism? Approaches to sex/gender in neuroscience. *Neuroethics*, 5(3): 305–15.

Kaiser, A., Haller, S., Schmitz, S., and Nitsch, C. (2009). On sex/gender related similarities and differences in fMRI language research. *Brain Research Reviews*, 61(2): 49–59.

Kaplan, J. M. (2010). When socially determined categories make biological realities. *The Monist*, 93(2): 283–99.

Kaplan, J. M. and Winther, R. G. (2013). Prisoners of abstraction? The theory and measure of genetic variation, and the very concept of "race." *Biological Theory*, 7(4): 401–12.

Kessler, S. J. (1990). The medical construction of gender: Case management of intersexed infants. *Signs: Journal of Women in Culture and Society*, 16(1): 3–26.

Kim, H. S. and Sasaki, J. Y. (2014). Cultural neuroscience: Biology of the mind in cultural contexts. *Annual Review of Psychology*, 65(1): 487–514.

Kitayama, S., Ishii, K., Imada, T., Takemura, K., and Ramaswamy, J. (2006). Voluntary settlement and the spirit of independence: Evidence from Japan's "northern frontier." *Journal of Personality and Social Psychology*, 91(3): 369–84.

Kitayama, S. and Park, J. (2010). Cultural neuroscience of the self: Understanding the social grounding of the brain. *Social Cognitive and Affective Neuroscience*, 5(2–3): 111–29.

Kõiv, R. (2023). Genetically caused trait is an interactive kind. *European Journal for Philosophy of Science*, 13(3): 31.

Kourany, J. A. (2010). *Philosophy of Science after Feminism*, Oxford: Oxford University Press.

Kronfeldner, M. (2018). *What's Left of Human Nature? A Post-Essentialist, Pluralist, and Interactive Account of a Contested Concept*, Cambridge, MA: MIT Press.

Kronfeldner, M., Roughley, N., and Toepfer, G. (2014). Recent work on human nature: Beyond traditional essences. *Philosophy Compass*, 9(9): 642–52.

Lester, B. M., Tronick, E., Nestler, E. et al. (2011). Behavioral epigenetics. *Annals of the New York Academy of Sciences*, 1226(1): 14–33.

Lewens, T. (2010). Foot note. *Analysis*, 70(3): 468–73.

Lewontin, R. C., Rose, S., and Kamin, L. (1984). *Not in Our Genes: Biology, Ideology, and Human Nature*, New York: Pantheon Books.

Lloyd, E. A. (1995). Objectivity and the double standard for feminist epistemologies. *Synthese*, 104(3): 351–81.

Longino, H. E. (1990). *Science as Social Knowledge: Values and Objectivity in Scientific Inquiry*, Princeton: Princeton University Press.

Losin, E. A. R., Dapretto, M., and Iacoboni, M. (2010). Culture and neuroscience: Additive or synergistic? *Social Cognitive and Affective Neuroscience*, 5(2–3): 148–58.

Mameli, M. (2024). *Why Human Nature Matters: Between Biology and Politics*, London: Bloomsbury.

Martínez Mateo, M., Cabanis, M., Loebell, N. C. d. E., and Krach, S. (2012). Concerns about cultural neurosciences: A critical analysis. *Neuroscience & Biobehavioral Reviews*, 36(1): 152–61.

Martínez Mateo, M., Cabanis, M., Stenmanns, J., and Krach, S. (2013). Essentializing the binary self: Individualism and collectivism in cultural neuroscience. *Frontiers in Human Neuroscience*, 7: 289.

Massa, M. G., Aghi, K., and Hill, M. J. (2023). Deconstructing sex: Strategies for undoing binary thinking in neuroendocrinology and behavior. *Hormones and Behavior*, 156: 105441.

Masuda, T., Batdorj, B., and Senzaki, S. (2020). Culture and attention: Future directions to expand research beyond the geographical regions of WEIRD cultures. *Frontiers in Psychology*, 11: 1394.

Masuda, T., Gonzalez, R., Kwan, L., and Nisbett, R. E. (2008). Culture and aesthetic preference: Comparing the attention to context of East Asians and Americans. *Personality and Social Psychology Bulletin*, 34(9): 1260–75.

Mayr, E. (1959). Darwin and the evolutionary theory in biology. In B. J. Meggers, ed., *Evolution and Anthropology: A Centennial Appraisal*. Washington, DC: Anthropological Society of Washington, pp. 1–10.

McCarthy, M. M., Arnold, A. P., Ball, G. F., Blaustein, J. D., and De Vries, G. J. (2012). Sex differences in the brain: The not so inconvenient truth. *Journal of Neuroscience*, 32(7): 2241–47.

McCarthy, M. M., Auger, A. P., Bale, T. L. et al. (2009). The epigenetics of sex differences in the brain. *Journal of Neuroscience*, 29(41): 12815–23.

McCarthy, M. M., Nugent, B. M., and Lenz, K. M. (2017). Neuroimmunology and neuroepigenetics in the establishment of sex differences in the brain. *Nature Reviews Neuroscience*, 18: 471.

McCauley, R. N. and Henrich, J. (2006). Susceptibility to the Müller-Lyer illusion, theory-neutral observation, and the diachronic penetrability of the visual input system. *Philosophical Psychology*, 19(1): 79–101.

McGowan, P. O., Sasaki, A., and Roth, T. L. (2014). The social environment and epigenetics in psychiatry. In J. Peedicayil, D. R. Grayson, and

D. Avramopoulos, eds., *Epigenetics in Psychiatry*. Boston, MA: Academic Press, pp. 547–62.

Meynell, L. (2020). What's wrong with (narrow) evolutionary psychology. In S. Crasnow and K. Intemann, eds., *The Routledge Handbook of Feminist Philosophy of Science*. New York: Routledge, pp. 303–15.

Millum, J. (2006). Natural goodness and natural evil. *Ratio*, 19(2): 199–213.

Müller, G. B. (2003). Embryonic motility: Environmental influences and evolutionary innovation. *Evolution & Development*, 5(1): 56–60.

Nado, J. (2021). Conceptual engineering, truth, and efficacy. *Synthese*, 198 (Suppl 7): S1507–S27.

Nelson, N. C. (2018). *Model Behavior: Animal Experiments, Complexity, and the Genetics of Psychiatric Disorders*, Chicago, IL: University of Chicago Press.

Nisbett, R. E. (2005). *The Geography of Thought: How Asians and Westerners Think Differently . . . and Why*, London: Nicholas Brealey.

(2009). *Intelligence and How to Get It: Why Schools and Cultures Count*, New York: W. W. Norton.

Nisbett, R. E., Peng, K., Choi, I., and Norenzayan, A. (2001). Culture and systems of thought: Holistic versus analytic cognition. *Psychological Review*, 108(2): 291–310.

Nussbaum, M. (2000). *Women and Human Development: The Capabilities Approach*, Cambridge: Cambridge University Press.

(2011). *Creating Capabilities: The Human Development Approach*, Cambridge, MA: Harvard University Press.

Odenbaugh, J. (2017). Nothing in ethics makes sense except in the light of evolution? Natural goodness, normativity, and naturalism. *Synthese*, 194(4): 1031–55.

Oliver, M. (1990). *The Politics of Disablement*, London: Macmillan.

Packer, M. J. and Cole, M. (2023). The challenges to the study of cultural variation in cognition. *Review of Philosophy and Psychology*, 14(2): 515–37.

Palmer, A. R. (2012). Developmental plasticity and the origin of novel forms: Unveiling cryptic genetic variation via "use and disuse." *Journal of Experimental Zoology Part B: Molecular and Developmental Evolution*, 318(6): 466–79.

Panofsky, A., Dasgupta, K., and Iturriaga, N. (2021). How White nationalists mobilize genetics: From genetic ancestry and human biodiversity to counterscience and metapolitics. *American Journal of Physical Anthropology*, 175(2): 387–98.

Pigliucci, M. (2001). *Phenotypic Plasticity: Beyond Nature and Nurture*, Baltimore, MD: Johns Hopkins University Press.

Pinker, S. A. (2002). *The Blank Slate: The Modern Denial of Human Nature*, New York: Viking Press.

Pinker, S. (2008). *The Sexual Paradox: Men, Women and the Real Gender Gap*, New York: Scribner.

Plaisance, K. S. and Elliott, K. C. (2021). A framework for analyzing broadly engaged philosophy of science. *Philosophy of Science*, 88(4): 594–615.

Potochnik, A. (2012). Feminist implications of model-based science. *Studies in History and Philosophy of Science*, 43(2): 383–89.

Powledge, T. M. (2011). Behavioral epigenetics: How nurture shapes nature. *BioScience*, 61(8): 588–92.

Quartz, S. R. (1999). The constructivist brain. *Trends in Cognitive Sciences*, 3(2): 48–57.

Qureshi, I. A. and Mehler, M. F. (2010). Genetic and epigenetic underpinnings of sex differences in the brain and in neurological and psychiatric disease susceptibility. In I. Savic, ed., *Sex Differences in the Human Brain, Their Underpinnings and Implications*. Amsterdam: Elsevier, pp. 77–95.

  (2014). An evolving view of epigenetic complexity in the brain. *Philosophical Transactions of the Royal Society B: Biological Sciences*, 369(1652): 20130506.

Ramsey, G. (2023). *Human Nature*, Cambridge: Cambridge University Press.

Read, J., Bentall, R. P., and Fosse, R. (2009). Time to abandon the bio-bio-bio model of psychosis: Exploring the epigenetic and psychological mechanisms by which adverse life events lead to psychotic symptoms. *Epidemiologia e Psichiatria Sociale*, 18(4): 299–310.

Richardson, R. C. (2007). *Evolutionary Psychology as Maladapted Psychology*, Cambridge, MA: MIT Press.

Richardson, S. S. (2017). Plasticity and programming: Feminism and the epigenetic imaginary. *Signs: Journal of Women in Culture and Society*, 43(1): 29–52.

  (2022). Sex contextualism. *Philosophy, Theory, and Practice in Biology*, 14: 2.

Ridley, R. (2019). Some difficulties behind the concept of the "Extreme male brain" in autism research. A theoretical review. *Research in Autism Spectrum Disorders*, 57: 19–27.

Rippon, G. (2019). *The Gendered Brain: The New Neuroscience that Shatters the Myth of the Female Brain*, London: Bodley Head.

Robert, J. (2004). *Embryology, Epigenesis, and Evolution: Taking Development Seriously*, Cambridge: Cambridge University Press.

Rouder, J. and Haaf, J. M. (2021). Are there reliable qualitative individual differences in cognition? *Journal of Cognition*, 4(1): 46.

Roughgarden, J. (2004). *Evolution's Rainbow: Diversity, Gender, and Sexuality in Nature and People*, Berkeley: University of California Press.

Ruigrok, A. N. V., Salimi-Khorshidi, G., Lai, M.-C. et al. (2014). A meta-analysis of sex differences in human brain structure. *Neuroscience & Biobehavioral Reviews*, 39: 34–50.

Rutten, B. P. F. and Mill, J. (2009). Epigenetic mediation of environmental influences in major psychotic disorders. *Schizophrenia Bulletin*, 35(6): 1045–56.

Sax, L. (2017). *Why Gender Matters: What Parents and Teachers Need to Know about the Emerging Science of Sex Differences, 2nd ed.*, New York: Harmony Books.

Schiebinger, L. (1999). *Has Feminism Changed Science?* Cambridge, MA: Harvard University Press.

Schienke, E. W., Baum, S. D., Tuana, N., Davis, K. J., and Keller, K. (2011). Intrinsic ethics regarding integrated assessment models for climate management. *Science and Engineering Ethics*, 17(3): 503–23.

Schulz, A. W. (2023). Explaining human diversity: The need to balance fit and complexity. *Review of Philosophy and Psychology*, 14(2): 457–75.

Seghier, M. L. and Price, C. J. (2018). Interpreting and utilising intersubject variability in brain function. *Trends in Cognitive Sciences*, 22(6): 517–30.

Shattuck-Heidorn, H. and Richardson, S. S. (2019). Sex/gender and the biosocial turn. *Scholar & Feminist Online*, 15(2). https://sfonline.barnard.edu/sex-gender-and-the-biosocial-turn.

Silvers, A. (1998). A fatal attraction to normalizing: Treating disabilities as deviations from "species-typical" functioning. In E. Parens, ed., *Enhancing Human Traits: Ethical and Social Implications*. Washington, DC: Georgetown University Press, pp. 95–123.

(2003). On the possibility and desirability of constructing a neutral conception of disability. *Theoretical Medicine and Bioethics*, 24(6): 471–87.

Smith, E. A. (2011). Endless forms: Human behavioural diversity and evolved universals. *Philosophical Transactions of the Royal Society B: Biological Sciences*, 366(1563): 325–32.

Snibbe, A. C. and Markus, H. R. (2005). You can't always get what you want: Educational attainment, agency, and choice. *Journal of Personality and Social Psychology*, 88(4): 703–20.

Sober, E. (1980). Evolution, population thinking, and essentialism. *Philosophy of Science*, 47(3): 350–83.

Springer, K. W., Stellman, J. M., and Jordan-Young, R. M. (2012). Beyond a catalogue of differences: A theoretical frame and good practice guidelines for researching sex/gender in human health. *Social Science & Medicine*, 74(11): 1817–24.

Stephens, N. M., Markus, H. R., and Townsend, S. S. M. (2007). Choice as an act of meaning: The case of social class. *Journal of Personality and Social Psychology*, 93(5): 814–30.

Stephens, N. M., Townsend, S. S. M., Markus, H. R., and Phillips, L. T. (2012). A cultural mismatch: Independent cultural norms produce greater increases in cortisol and more negative emotions among first-generation college students. *Journal of Experimental Social Psychology*, 48(6): 1389–93.

Sterelny, K. (2012). *The Evolved Apprentice*, Cambridge, MA: MIT Press.

(2018). Skeptical reflections on human nature. In E. Hannon and T. Lewens, eds., *Why We Disagree about Human Nature*. Oxford: Oxford University Press, pp. 108–26.

Stotz, K. (2006). With "genes" like that, who needs an environment? Postgenomics's argument for the "ontogeny of information." *Philosophy of Science*, 73(5): 905–17.

Stotz, K. and Griffiths, P. E. (2018). A developmental systems account of human nature. In E. Hannon and T. Lewens, eds., *Why We Disagree about Human Nature*. Oxford: Oxford University Press, pp. 58–75.

Suárez, J. (2023a). Masking, extrinsicness, and the nature of dispositions: The role of niche signals in muscle stem cells. *European Journal for Philosophy of Science*, 13(2): 21.

(2023b). What is the nature of stem cells? A unified dispositional framework. *Biology & Philosophy*, 38(5): 43.

Sultan, S. E. (2015). *Organism and Environment: Ecological Development, Niche Construction, and Adaptation*, Oxford: Oxford University Press.

Tabery, J. (2023). *Tyranny of the Gene: Personalized Medicine and Its Threat to Public Health*, New York: Knopf.

Tang, Y., Zhang, W., Chen, K. et al. (2006). Arithmetic processing in the brain shaped by cultures. *Proceedings of the National Academy of Sciences*, 103(28): 10775–80.

The Gurian Institute, Bering, S., and Goldberg, A. (2009). *It's a Baby Girl! The Unique Wonder and Special Nature of Your Daughter from Pregnancy to Two Years*, San Francisco, CA: Jossey-Bass.

Thompson, M. (1995). The representation of life. In R. Hursthouse, G. Lawrence, and W. Quinn, eds., *Virtues and Reasons: Philippa Foot and Moral Theory*. Oxford: Oxford University Press, pp. 206–46.

(2008). *Life and Action: Elementary Structures of Practice and Practical Thought*, Cambridge, MA: Harvard University Press.

Tomasello, M. (2019). *Becoming Human: A Theory of Ontogeny*, Cambridge, MA: Belknap Press.

Tooby, J. and Cosmides, L. (2015). Conceptual foundations of evolutionary psychology. In D. M. Buss, ed., *The Handbook of Evolutionary Psychology.* Hoboken: John Wiley & Sons, pp. 5–67.

Tooley, U. A., Bassett, D. S., and Mackey, A. P. (2021). Environmental influences on the pace of brain development. *Nature Reviews Neuroscience,* 22(6): 372–84.

Toyokawa, S., Uddin, M., Koenen, K. C., and Galea, S. (2012). How does the social environment "get into the mind?" Epigenetics at the intersection of social and psychiatric epidemiology. *Social Science & Medicine,* 74(1): 67–74.

Tramacere, A. and Bickle, J. (2024). *Neuro*epigenetics in philosophical focus: A critical analysis of the philosophy of mechanisms. *Biological Theory,* 19(1): 57–71.

Tremain, S. L., ed. (2023). *The Bloomsbury Guide to Philosophy of Disability,* London: Bloomsbury.

Uddin, M., Bustamante, A., and Toyokawa, S. (2014). Epigenetic epidemiology of psychiatric disorders. In J. Peedicayil, D. R. Grayson, and D. Avramopoulos, eds., *Epigenetics in Psychiatry.* Boston, MA: Academic Press, pp. 101–27.

Ursache, A. and Noble, K. G. (2016). Neurocognitive development in socioeconomic context: Multiple mechanisms and implications for measuring socioeconomic status. *Psychophysiology,* 53(1): 71–82.

Uskul, A. K., Kitayama, S., and Nisbett, R. E. (2008). Ecocultural basis of cognition: Farmers and fishermen are more holistic than herders. *Proceedings of the National Academy of Sciences,* 105(25): 8552–56.

Valian, V. (2014). Interests, gender, and science. *Perspectives on Psychological Science,* 9(2): 225–30.

Valles, S. A. (2019). *Philosophy of Population Health: Philosophy for a New Public Health Era,* New York: Routledge.

(2021). A pluralistic and socially responsible philosophy of epidemiology field should actively engage with social determinants of health and health disparities. *Synthese,* 198(10): 2589–611.

van Anders, S. M. (2013). Beyond masculinity: Testosterone, gender/sex, and human social behavior in a comparative context. *Frontiers in Neuroendocrinology,* 34(3): 198–210.

(2015). Beyond sexual orientation: Integrating gender/sex and diverse sexualities via sexual configurations theory. *Archives of Sexual Behavior,* 44(5): 1177–213.

van Anders, S. M., Schudson, Z. C., Abed, E. C. et al. (2017). Biological sex, gender, and public policy. *Policy Insights from the Behavioral and Brain Sciences,* 4(2): 194–201.

van Anders, S. M., Steiger, J., and Goldey, K. L. (2015). Effects of gendered behavior on testosterone in women and men. *Proceedings of the National Academy of Sciences*, 112(45): 13805–10.

Vickers, A. L. and Kitcher, P. (2003). Pop sociobiology reborn: The evolutionary psychology of sex and violence. In C. B. Travis, ed., *Evolution, Gender, and Rape*. Cambridge, MA: MIT Press, pp. 139–68.

Vogeley, K. and Roepstorff, A. (2009). Contextualising culture and social cognition. *Trends in Cognitive Sciences*, 13(12): 511–6.

Walker, N. (2021a). A horizon of possibility: Some notes on neuroqueer theory. In N. Walker, ed., *Neuroqueer Heresies: Notes on the Neurodiversity Paradigm, Autistic Empowerment, and Postnormal Possibilities*. Fort Worth, TX: Autonomous Press, pp. 169–91.

   (2021b). *Neuroqueer Heresies: Notes on the Neurodiversity Paradigm, Autistic Empowerment, and Postnormal Possibilities*, Fort Worth, TX: Autonomous Press.

Walker, I. and Read, J. (2002). The differential effectiveness of psychosocial and biogenetic causal explanations in reducing negative attitudes toward "mental illness." *Psychiatry: Interpersonal and Biological Processes*, 65(4): 313–25.

Wang, G., Mao, L., Ma, Y. et al. (2012). Neural representations of close others in collectivistic brains. *Social Cognitive and Affective Neuroscience*, 7(2): 222–29.

Ward, Z. B. (2022). Cognitive variation: The philosophical landscape. *Philosophy Compass*, 17(10): e12882.

Wasserman, D. and Aas, S. (2023). Disability: Definitions and models. In E. N. Zalta and U. Nodelman, eds., *The Stanford Encyclopedia of Philosophy, Fall 2023 edition*. https://plato.stanford.edu/archives/fall2023/entries/disability/.

Weaver, S. (2017). *A Constructive Critical Assessment of Feminist Evolutionary Psychology*, Dissertation, University of Waterloo. https://hdl.handle.net/10012/12772.

West-Eberhard, M. J. (2003). *Developmental Plasticity and Evolution*, Oxford: Oxford University Press.

Whitman, D. W. and Agrawal, A. A. (2009). What is phenotypic plasticity and why is it important? In D. W. Whitman and T. N. Ananthakrishnan, eds., *Phenotypic Plasticity of Insects: Mechanisms and Consequences*. Enfield: Science, pp. 1–63.

Woodcock, S. (2006). Philippa Foot's virtue ethics has an Achilles' heel. *Dialogue: Canadian Philosophical Review / Revue canadienne de philosophie*, 45(3): 445–68.

Wouters, A. (2003). Four notions of biological function. *Studies in History and Philosophy of Biological and Biomedical Sciences*, 34(4): 633–68.

Wylie, A. and Hankinson Nelson, L. (2007). Coming to terms with the values of science: Insights from feminist science scholarship. In H. Kincaid, J. Dupré, and A. Wylie, eds., *Value-Free Science? Ideals and Illusions*. Oxford: Oxford University Press, pp. 58–86.

Zawidzki, T. W. (2013). *Mindshaping: A New Framework for Understanding Human Social Cognition*, Cambridge, MA: MIT Press.

Zhang, L., Zhou, T., Zhang, J. et al. (2006). In search of the Chinese self: An fMRI study. *Science in China Series C*, 49(1): 89–96.

Acknowledgements

I am greatly indebted to two anonymous reviewers for their comments on a whole draft of this Element. For discussions on individual aspects of this research project, I thank the Fall 2022 Visiting Fellows at the Center for Philosophy of Science of the University of Pittsburgh, the members of PhilBio group at the University of Bielefeld, and the audiences at the meetings of the *Canadian Society for the History and Philosophy Science*, the *International Society for the History, Philosophy and Social Studies of Biology*, the *Philosophy of Science Association*, and the *Society for Philosophy of Science in Practice*. The work on this project was supported by the Social Sciences and Humanities Research Council of Canada (Insight Grant 435–2016–0500) and the Canada Research Chairs Program (CRC-2018–00052).

Cambridge Elements ≡

Philosophy of Biology

Grant Ramsey
KU Leuven

Grant Ramsey is a BOFZAP research professor at the Institute of Philosophy, KU Leuven, Belgium. His work centers on philosophical problems at the foundation of evolutionary biology. He has been awarded the Popper Prize twice for his work in this area. He also publishes in the philosophy of animal behavior, human nature and the moral emotions. He runs the Ramsey Lab (theramseylab.org), a highly collaborative research group focused on issues in the philosophy of the life sciences.

About the Series

This Cambridge Elements series provides concise and structured introductions to all of the central topics in the philosophy of biology. Contributors to the series are cutting-edge researchers who offer balanced, comprehensive coverage of multiple perspectives, while also developing new ideas and arguments from a unique viewpoint.

Printed by Integrated Books International,
United States of America